Cusp/detritus

EAST VANCOUVER ALLEYWAY

Cusp/detritus:
an experiment in alleyways

POETRY BY *Catherine Owen*

PHOTOGRAPHS BY *Karen Moe*

ANVIL PRESS | VANCOUVER

Cusp/detritus
Copyright © 2006 by Catherine Owen | Photographs Copyright © 2006 by Karen Moe

All rights reserved. No part of this book may be reproduced by any means without the prior written permission of the publisher, with the exception of brief passages in reviews. Any request for photocopying or other reprographic copying of any part of this book must be directed in writing to access: The Canadian Copyright Licensing Agency, One Yonge Street, Suite 1900, Toronto, Ontario, Canada, M5E 1E5.

NATIONAL LIBRARY OF CANADA CATALOGUING IN PUBLICATION DATA

Owen, Catherine, 1971-
    Cusp/detritus: an experiment in alleyways / Catherine Owen.

Poems.

ISBN 1-895636-74-4

    I. Title.

PS8579.W43C88 2006   C811'.54   C2006-905159-3

Printed and bound in Canada
Cover design: Typesmith Design
Cover image: "Child's Suitcase" by Karen Moe
Typesetting & Interior Design: HeimatHouse
Photo of Frank Bonneville: Gary Desjardins
Photo of Catherine Owen & Karen Moe: Gerald Owen

Represented in Canada by the Literary Press Group
Distributed by the University of Toronto Press

NOTE: This book is a work of both non-fiction and the imagination—all names of those still living have been changed.

The publisher gratefully acknowledges the financial assistance of the Canada Council for the Arts, the Book Publishing Industry Development Program (BPIDP), and the Province of British Columbia through the B.C. Arts Council and the Book Publishing Tax Credit.

Anvil Press
P.O. Box 3008, Main Post Office
Vancouver, B.C. V6B 3X5 CANADA
www.anvilpress.com

for
Frank Bonneville, dark angel

1974 – 2003

> *O, the beautiful nothing of madness!*
> —Randall Deere,
> Commercial Drive, 2001

> *With death we have one recourse: to make art before it*
> —René Char

> *I do not fear that I will go mad but that I may not/*
> *And the shadows of my sanity blacken out*
> *Your burning*
> —Gwendolyn McEwen

> *Soyez maudits, d'abord d'ètre ce que vous ètes/et*
> *Puis soyez maudits d'obsèder les poètes!*
> —Victor Hugo

Table of Contents

peripheral visions: a preface   9

Coroner's Report   14
The Midwife   17
Exhibits A, B, X   19
current   23
instability   25
squat   26
Once Upon a Space   29
The Astronomy Lesson   31
The Year of the Snake   32
swarm   34
Open Letter to a Black Hole   38
No Water but Rock   40
dyslexic   42
remnants   44
Dialogue for One Voice   45
The Hitler Room   48
recovery   51
temperature   54
eidolon   56
essay   57
A Remedial Post-Mortem   58
jagged   60
feather   62

The Curator 63
list 66
itinerant 75
asp 76
nathan 78
barred 80
dismantling 81
Empty Landscapes of Psychosis 83
delusions 85
drought 87
A Glosa on Four First Lines by Siegfried Sassoon 88
Tai-Chi on the Psych Ward, with Frank 90
Un Patient est Trouvé Mort: Haikus from the French 91
fix 93
The Laying Out: A Glosa on Lines from Osip Mandelstam 94
The Mourners 97
Gallery: Anti-sonnets 98
The Ward 103

End Notes 113
Acknowledgments 116
Afterword 117
About the Author & the Photographer 119

peripheral visions: a preface

June 6, 2006
RICHMOND, BC

I wake, guilt smashing against my mind's breakwaters. I have no right to be the author of this book. The cold mouth of my imagination I called holy and that devoured all those lives. I am a cannibal of unhappiness. The pure intentions and politicized impact I've been elaborating around this project seem as much a sham as everything else that surrounds the fuck, shit, puke and rot at the core of being human. My morbid obsession, Frank called it—is it little more than this?

    As I stare at the man by my side, the man who has carried me through so much grieving, he turns into the muse I lost. Crazy.

    Like the tell-tale heart bashing beneath the floorboards of a body, his eyes shift from generous brown to a chilly green, flicked with a gold I cannot mine anymore, accusatory in their deadness? Or just dead? Art should never apologize. Sorry this morning anyway. So sorry.

August 8, 1999
COMMERCIAL DRIVE, VANCOUVER, BC

Been living here for a month now, in a basement suite off the renegade alley that spines between the sedate trees of Victoria Drive and the Van East Theatre, currently showing *Three Seasons* at 4:30 and 7:00. From there, I take my daily walk towards Hastings, stop for an espresso at Coloreia, pass the squat beside Café Deux's reggae and cream cheese muffins, the barbershop on 1st beneath Karen's, by Wazuubee's where long ago Chad and I were poets in residence for twenty-five bucks and a plate of garlic mayo fries, beneath

Beckwoman's beads and Bolshevik posters, glancing at Co-op Books across the street, Highlife Records, the Fig Mart, deke through the scruff of Grandview Park, Mecca's vintage, Joe's rainbow mug, then Attic Treasures, Zesty's and the street ends for me there, at Venables, before the #20's curve towards the Bollywood theatre and down past The Waldorf to Burrard's salty mountains. Life has become a play—theme and variations—which every day is enacted by Manny & Dara, Mr. Socks, Stirstick, Jitterboy, Randall Deere, the Spoon Man, The Cowpoke and Mr Smiley Guy.

   I am drawn by those who completely inhabit this environment, scavenge its spaces, all its dumpsters, alcoves, cheap eats, bushes and gathering spots mapped out, diligent and essential. The illusion of ownership has not been lost; it has become liquid, flooding this urban terrain with cigarette butts, take-out noodles, needles, unleashing laughter, rotten teeth, rage, wilted lettuce, paper cups and hands, hands, hands, lifting in a slap and a caress to the coins that dance their way down.

November 19, 1999

Today I bought a greasy breakfast for Randall Deere so I could take pictures of him scrawling his schizophrenic visions into a spiral notebook; then, going home by Juicy Lucy's I spied Jitterboy spinning his last smoke into the street and I followed him, at a distance, but still, all the way to his house at the top of 6th, staring at his black stride taking the alleys hard, dark hair fluttering. I keep thinking that if I spend enough time with them, watching, listening, then not only will poems emerge but they will be valid, honest, and worth the utter mess I'm making of my marriage, so obsessed I can't eat out anymore without abandoning Chad to pursue one of my characters, always in the hopes they'll yield the revelatory impossible.

   The worst mistake I've made so far was with Nathan, allowing a few chats about Dostoyevsky while he munched the sweet & sour pork I'd bought him to turn into a kiss and an invitation to see The Damned. When I went to pick him up, we had to walk all over town to find a place in which to lodge his dog, Pariah, then to hook him up with his dealer, and the band had just taken the stage when he vanished, patched pants incongruous in the revamped Commodore.

And like some kind of possessed detective, I keep my mind on traces, follow remnants.

July 23, 2000

As soon as he threw open the door at Corazon, the after-hours salon Karen's been running out of her 1st Ave apartment, and dashed his eyes against me like the blind, I realized that all I had experienced until now of obsession and occult attachment was a pale rumble to a full-bore storm. With zombie devotion, I left when he left, not with him, but behind him, as an unwanted Euridice, floating into his hell.

October 18, 2000

The garbage strike's been going on for weeks now and the refuse in the alleys has mounted from curio to monstrosity. Karen's begun to chronicle my findings from mornings of alley walks: a pill bottle's collapsed lung, a truck overwhelmed by ivy, a discarded toilet she snapped, crashed on her stomach to capture the most lyrical angle. Frank's gone back to Montreal and, in his absence, poems punch their way out of me, confused, delirious, not the shapely melancholy of the ghazals I've been writing for him in *Shall*, but a noisy, bruised assemblage of prose pieces, his memory the mad king in a mad court of voices.

November 2000, May 2001, February 2002
MONTREAL, QB

The first time I visit him his uncle asks me, as we sit scarfing poutine at La Belle Province, "So what do you see in Frankie?"

The second time I visit him we break open a hundred fortune cookies, lying on his mattress in St. Henri and read none of them.

The third time I visit him he gets a day pass from the psych ward and, after my reading from *The Wrecks of Eden* at The Yellow Door whispers, "You're gorgeous." It is the most terrible thing he has ever said to me.

March 1, 2003

R. called today. And because he couldn't say the word dead, I didn't understand what he was trying to tell me. They found him. In the parking lot. His body was perfect. Not a mark on him. *Is he injured?* I asked.

March 24, 2003

The day after I return from the funeral, I find the theatre chairs with the squeegee hanging off one of the wooden backs. Call Karen, excited, and demand she drop everything to snap them. Been crying for weeks, silenced. Now I feel the book is blessed in some mysterious way, enabled again. Poems re-enter me, turning towards tradition's forms; the body that refused his proposal marrying him through glosas, sonnets. Karen making the run-over suitcase beautiful, dark eyes of last Fall's apples in a shopping cart, shoals of records in an eviction pile. I hug Randall Deere in front of Fet's, in love with the street again.

Its ghosts & flesh.

December, 2004

Karen responds to a technical question: "The biggest challenge of shooting this series? It has to be gravel. Definitely hard to aestheticize. Yup."

April, 2005

Catherine drafts an artist's statement: "Politically, I hope *Cusp* honours the rejected, renders them visible, humanizing homelessness, addiction, schizophrenia. Poetically, as always, I need to know I'm revivifying language, bleeding new rhythms, metaphors into the world. And, in the process, I want the book to serve as tribute, apology, epitaph for the Muse I lost along the way."

June 7, 2006

The catalogue arrives in the mail. Finally. Seven years since I began writing the poems, six years since commencing the collaboration with Karen, three years since Frank's death completed this blood-book, leaving my longing forever unfinished, I turn it over in my hands.

Coroner's Report

For Frank Bonneville, dead at 28
August 11/74 – March 1/03

A man was found.
There were no signs as to what, if anything.

The traces were there, but nobody had taken
the trouble, amidst the pieces of then and now,
to

There had been some concern as to a pattern
of recurrence but it was only like night coming,
inevitable

A form was left at the nurses' desk, signed
by his hand and signaling a process, the gears
of which, when set into motion

He wore a winter coat, meaning it was cold; a
harmonica was found in his pocket, meaning
the desire to be musical; seven tattoos could be
seen, one of them only half of the word *love*,
meaning

They had already decided there was no particular
combination of pills; no regime; no fail-proof
course of action to forestall this,
falling

In the hospital's asphalt shadow, a limb,
a gesture as though to prevent (the imagination's
need for the accidental), as though it were

And thus he left no survivors, the light
obliterating his photos

There were some openly relieved while others
in their grieving clenched a secret core of breath,
said

Yet who has witnessed another such life
dedicated to the pursuit of

The cause of death: death

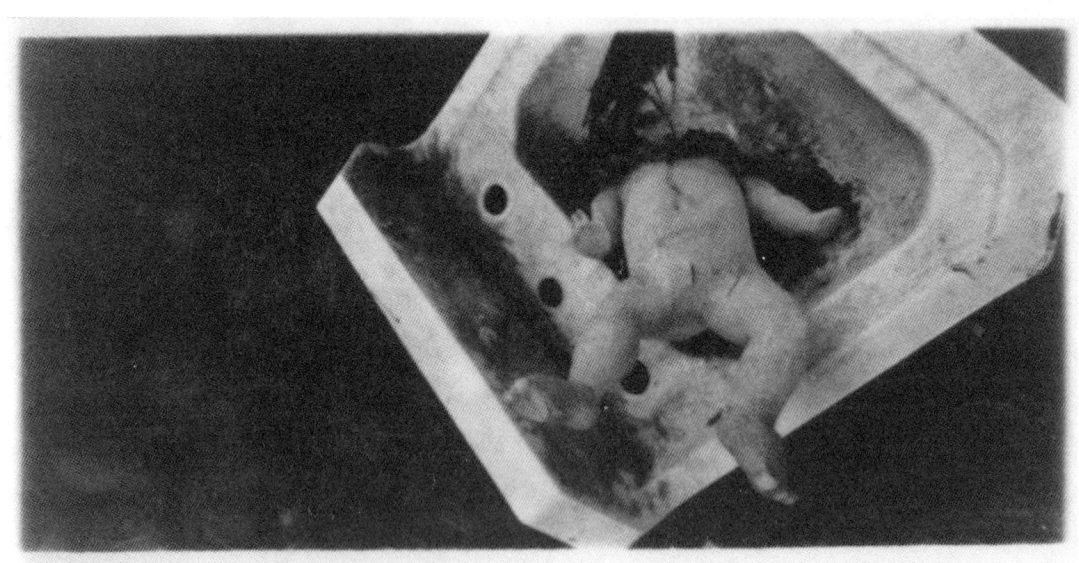

SINK-BABY

The Midwife

His eyes are long and almond and like the almond always seem to carry their shell. Terse veins run the breadth of his arms, one the clenched stretch of his cheekbone. An inch-long nick bisects the line of his neck like a silent, persistent mouth.

How old d'you think I am, lady?

It is her fault for seeking him in data: age, place of birth, number of siblings. Who has she ever found in this way? He is the most amiable, intense panhandler on the street, striding up to passersby with a "Hey, blood" and, if ignored, still bowing to them as they walk by, "Peace, eh." When she first met him he was holding court on the corner by the pasta store, raging tales of his parentage—

Do you know how hard it was growing up as John Deere's son? All the tractor parts lying around in the yard and the Buddha watching everything, shaking his head. The nurses just couldn't believe it, man. I was born so small, one of four Chinese brothers, curved sideways, like this, and with a silver chain in my hand, the cord like a lion's tail around my throat...

You understand, these are not statistics. The only information she has been able to glean from him is his name and it is almost too common to be worthwhile.

He is beautiful when he opens around this syllable, this reminder of a distant christening. She longs to speak it again and again, as if to draw him out of his mind's dark well and into flesh, youth, embrace. When they caress after she presses coins into his hand, clad in a cyclist's glove or ridged with the washers he wears as rings, she tells him—*you are the only one I can't resist*. She has to be careful of such declarations.

Now they are sitting across from each other in the spare confines of the Cottage Restaurant where she has ordered him sausage and eggs so that he will stay still long enough to recount his narratives of another country—

This meat, he says, prodding at the greasy length, *came from a blue pine. Look you can tell by the grain of its skin, and this, this is a moon-egg whose roots reach back to the medicine plants of the elders. It's the truth. I used to be a Krishna and sell thousands of them a day. That was before I started delivering babies in the compound at VGH where the doctors carry M-42's. Clones, all of them. It's totally crazy the warping power of chromosomes and kinetic forces . . .*

How tenderly he wraps each bite of food in a blanket of bread before placing it on his incessant tongue.

Something always moving in her that she can't account for.

Exhibits

A / *To live in the world as if in an immense museum of strangeness*
—Giorgio de Chirico

A certain inflection on the word you is what she first knows him by. As if the word were a resistant material he had to press into cognizance by this emphasis in his voice. *Can you spare a coin?* Steel receiving the faintest imprint of heat. Once he told her his name, on a stray evening in November, and now every time she meets him, the dark haunt in his eyelids like Durer's doomed owl, she speaks it—*Hey* ___. Have you ever seen the film lift off the flesh of the dying? One syllable can waken more than a whole lifetime of speech. The baptism of ___ between Continental and Starbucks, outside Figmart, or on the shadow where the hanged painter used to unfold his easel and dog for the duration of Sundays. (Yet sound dries so quickly; naming dissolves). Drunk, she hugged him, mid-lope, one night and afterwards wrote in a letter, as though despairingly: *I can never become an artifact to him, or a familiar. Magritte's transparencies approximate—how bones are a cove for stars or forests. He has no means to connect to me—knowing the filaments of identity are unbearably thin. That Ovid was only elaborating common occurrences.*

B / *The singular aura of alienness that hovers around them*
—Louis Sass

There is in his posture an assumption: notice the hand pincered on one hip, its tiny jutting, while the other suspends the cigarette in a V, an obstructed peace sign. A gaze is not sufficient. Stare until the comforts of narrative dissolve and all you are left with is a thread dangling from the cuff of his night-black Army & Navy shirt, swaying slightly like a thin worm. His movements are more predictable than the weather. In the small café he spins on the stool, stirs his coffee, crosses & uncrosses his pared-down legs in an inner game of chess in which there is never any checkmate, never any relief from the machinery of his flesh. Once she asked for the time and watched his mouth open like a globe. *No*, he said, and then again, *no*. A whisper out of all correspondence with the deafening, irrelevant requests of the world.

x / *He may no longer seem to have a soul and may treat you like an utter stranger*
—Louis Sass

When she left him and moved back to her father's small walk-up on the Plat, half a country away, his friends all dubbed her *that little shit* and refused to eat at the restaurant where she used to waitress. He mailed her shards of narrative: "Lefty Luciano and his Whore," "Bitty, the Cunt-Queen of Commercial Drive," or the erratic serial, "Young, dumb and full of cum." He asked her to critique the concreteness of the dialogue. He asked her to consider possible conclusions. She wrote back, furious, *Couldn't you say you love and miss me?*

Couldn't you say hate?

§

In routine activities, he is beautiful. Reaching in Alain's fridge for the tabasco and cream, for Polish sausage and the silver luxury of brie, sleeves rolled to the elbow, singing a Danzig tune like Billie Holiday, he shines. Cooking, washing the landlord's car, even cutting his toenails, there is a temporary cauterization. The voices that leak like blood into his mind dry around such duties. Once I was giving him head, his cock curving its distance into my body, when Alain pounded on the door: *The toilet. It's overflowing. Get up.* He tore himself from me with a painful eagerness, returning bright with the momentary glow of this rescue. I understood then that my tongue silenced nothing. That his respite was in the necessity of chains & cogs, porcelain places.

§

Years later, you remember standing in La Gare waiting for him and seeing him walk towards you—intense slouch, hands punched in pockets—seeing him walk past you, towards the sliding glass doors, unseeing you, and you having no choice but to follow, treading to the left of the thread he tightropes, taut with orders whose echoes ebb around you until he turns again into self—or some approximate conversation with things—one of which, on the cilia of his eye, you were, waiting in La Gare's crowded embrace.

DREAMER/DECEIVER

current

If, as Heraclitus said, it is death for souls to become water, then you are no longer living. Sitting on the corner of Venables or 3rd or in front of the liquor store by the man with the somnolent puppets and the girl selling piercings, you flood the street with the tiny leakage of your voice, your eyes' alluvial gaze.

> *Can you spare some change, miss?*
> *Charming boy—says he wants some food...*
> *Get a blow-job, ass-face!*
> *Here, buy some gloves with this, a buck at Liberties,*
> *your hands are blue...*
>
> *My hands are blue...I want to die...if I could only get to a*
> *photocopier...if things wouldn't be lost in fires, as puke rags,*
> *in squats raided by pigs...*

In the desert, there are mirages that lead travelers to think they have found water, a quavering haze that promises speech and delivers only the greater silence of mistaken appearances. In the city, the mirages are accretions of dust and cement, refuse and asphalt. They seem certain, water's antitheses. If you touch them, however, after a long life's crawling, you will find them wet, viscous with a wrinkling moisture. Believing in the dry solidity of things will become an unbearable fantasy after this.

> *Fuckin-A! Don't you love the sound of it!*
> *See what I've written, round and round, upside down...*
> *Can you spare some change, sir?*

*Take these pills to stop the night sweats and this one
for nausea, this for fear, ok?*

*I'm scared...I want to die...just dematerialize for a while,
you know...be not here, a day or more...*

When you offer me your journal, I see that the pages are damp, the spine weighed with forays beneath the ocean. There are stories of vomit. Sputum rests in a small target mark by one of the margins. A drawing shows you bent over a syringe, naked, while a man fat as land laps at your rectum. *Slurp, slurp,* speaks the bubble above his tongue.

Now I resist you on the street as a drowner repelling a whirlpool. Your salt. Blue pupils. Lucretius. His widening noose of seeds.

instability

The fibrillation of his hands on the colander as he carried it towards her, a nine-months' womb of pears. Not the Bartletts she was accustomed to, but seeds from the Orient he had woven into the earth fifteen years ago when he, his wife, and five sons named after notes (Re, Mi, Fa, So and La) had arrived from Malaysia. This fruit was, in shape, more like an apple, yet cratered with indentations like the pads of fingertips. A coarse, chamois-coloured skin that, he said, in his voice which murmured in a fierce almost-sleepfulness, should be peeled, *like this*, his wrist quavering, curling in the autumn garden air. The insides, she knew, would be pale as soy milk, flecked with minute freckles, and taut. Would taste more of lychee nuts than the pears she was used to from the asphalt-tree of her childhood. Like the nuts he had once peeled for her with the curt, determined spasms of his clean, doctored fingers until the sweet, jellied globe had appeared. An eye blind to his hands like earthquakes on her flesh.

squat

holy, holy, holy the girl is saying. over the candle. its three flames. on the ceiling, simon's shadow crustacean as he tightens the strap around his bicep, holds his arm taut, flicks and flicks the raised scar of a vein. luke is already jonesing. his body on the sleeping bag shudders, tosses. the girl can see the sweat riding the rims of the pimples on his forehead, strange drawings of snowmen. oh, god, the girl is new to this, but nonchalant seeming, lotus-legged on the blankets the boys had layered for her between them so she could get some sleep. *sleep, fuck,* she keeps saying to herself, *sleep, fuck,* her breath white as a flame huffing out of her and luke scrunching up stuff and simon calling, *watch me for a minute, will ya, somebody watch me!* the girl *is* watching, the thin body of the needle penetrating, but this is not what he wants. *luke wouldya?* desperate now. pleading. double quick luke's hand—*shit stinks!*—and the ashtray, flying saucer, smashes—*goddamit!*—on the far wall, shards like a sharp snow, coming down. *Whydyoudothatman?* simon, his legs lengthening away from him, falls then. backward on his mat, on writing book, *Gravity's Rainbow* thumbed badly and the avocado pit carved like a shaman he bought for his brother's birthday. luke is laughing, hooting—*jesus crisp*—turning to the girl, *hey, sorry about the temper thing. d'you know I've been with my girl for eleven years? pretty good, eh, and I'm only 26. well, we're not together now, 'cause she's in Vernon working at the d.q. and I'm trying to get shit happening here, squeegying and stuff...d'you believe in aliens?* wiggling her fingers in the afghan's itchy holes—*yeah sorta.*

you gotta, he says, *it's proven. you know how many times I've seen ufo's?* she's seen him sometimes on the drive wearing a tee beneath the long chrysalis of his backpack. two cartoon martians screwing with the caption—*aliens are coming!* her fingers wiggle at him. *oh, right, you came here to sleep, get away kinda thing—old man?* her lids have a fire beneath them. she nods. says nothing.

simon rises then, abrupt, rustles in the bike parts, cans, for coins it seems as soon—*soda anyone? I'm going out. candy bar, lukeish? make mine a Snickers*, says luke, then, once simon's gone, checking for cops, inching through the gouge in the fence, turns to the girl—*gone to score again for sure.* the girl's voice coming out plaintive—*you mean, you won't get your Snickers?*

traffic around them. room-smell of socks, punk leather, flicker of flesh. luke shifts in his sleeping bag to stare at her, the tiny darks of his eyes, tells her when he used to rise to coffee perking, before the first rig and the bugs, before they started living in every damned hole he has—*care to watch me jack off?* he says, face like a wick, passive.

    §

near daylight, the girl slips out to pee, crouching the two scars of her thighs over the asphalt runnel alongside the squat, letting the stream penetrate newspapers, bottles. in the sky, the moon's pale arm extends itself amid the new blue of morning and gulls wheel inhuman, wheel and wheel.

SQUEEGEE

Once Upon a Space

It was happening again. Empty. Full. Full. Empty. The expenditures of her body in yet another futile act.

The doctor is unhealthily handsome. Sloshing a stick around in her pale, innocent urine, he makes a positive hieroglyph on the chart, asks her with a regulation face—

Have you thought about birth control?

IUDs cascading from the sky like so much medieval candy—*All our nurses have them.* 21- or 28-day pills—*But seven of them are sugar.* The cap she can fit into her cervix full of gel—a sperm's suicidal choice. And what if her tubes are cauterized? *A simple procedure.* Condoms thinning and tearing in the world's hastening decay.

My husband has had a vasectomy. But this is not my husband's.

It had been a transcendental incident. Drunk, high, and with two men inside her. Every hole that could leak her hollowness to the room, filled. She even thought she was loved in this excess of tongues and arms, of thin, plunging cocks. To be overtaken was to be loved, was it not? To have no breath left to utter anything otherwise.

That is a problem, he carries on, flipping backwards through her chart, its shattered narration. *It's a straightforward surgery, but the choice is always difficult...*

Her face looks at him with the blunt silencing of a deeper authority. All the sounds of aspiration machines, the feel of needles penetrating flesh, antiseptic rooms, legs opening into absence like a child's drawing of birds—all this gathers into her gaze.

Yes, well—I'll get you the numbers.

Empty. Full. Full. Empty. She places her hand over her womb at night as though over yet another mouth trying to speak in a tongue, archaic and irretrievable.

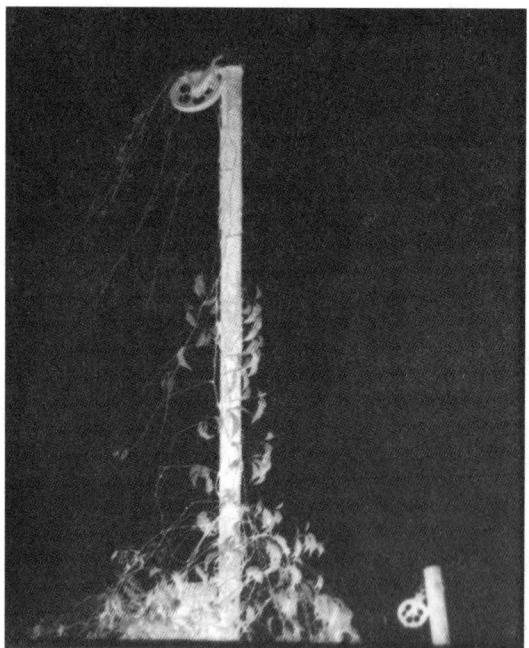

IVY CLOTHESLINES

The Astronomy Lesson

They were laughing when the cramps began. Black Sabbath on the stereo and dope in their lungs, crazy laughing at the black marriage of their lives. Earlier that day, she had swallowed the pills that would put an end to the dark, ambiguous swarm of cells suspended in her womb—on the ultrasound it was a gray space swimming with static, tissue. She had known for a month now that the stranger's child was growing within her, spreading a hot sleep over her mind. At first, she had been rabid about keeping it, piqued at the thought of birthing a child whose father was as detached from her as the farthest planet from the sun. Pregnancy had always terrified her with the implications of its entanglements. This child—not of love, not of domesticity, but of a momentary unraveling with a nameless man—would be free of this burden.

Of course, her husband had been of a different mind, and so she had kept the appointment.

In the bathroom, her womb tightened mildly, like a child's fist over a finger and, tiny but palpable, the fetus slid out of her and into the cold waters. There was no cry inside her. *Spoon, spoon*, she called.

Once she had found a dead hummingbird in the yard and had kept it for the innocence of its iridescent wings. Within days, however, it had been indistinguishable from any other death save for the sharpness of its beak, its infinite smallness. She slid the fetus off the wet pool of steel and into the box that had held their wedding rings. Ozzy sang *Paranoid* and *Dirty Women* in the smoky background.

Over the week, it hardened on its mossy bier into a spine of red amber. It could have been any species really, she thought from time to time, opening the lid to wonder at it. Its head and hands and feet only points on an unfinished and forever distant star.

The Year of the Snake

It was afterwards and they were out on the pavement, Ashley, Bauble, and the little girl. Ashley's face was bleeding, thin traces of it wending through his uneven beard which looked as if it had been erased in several places. The child, who was theirs and not theirs, picked steadily at the cork from the champagne bottle, making a tiny snow of pellets around her feet. *Hey*, Ashley nudged her, his voice coming out swollen, *don't waste those things. Soon, before you're big, they'll be plastic. Those cork trees, man, will be gone, gone, gone.* The child echoed his last word, dropping its syllable around her feet in a tiny snow of sound. Bauble slapped her then, one quick clap and it was quiet. Cars spun around them like a metal storm.

Bauble caressed her ribs with one hand. *Baby, I think they're broken.* Moaning to Ashley who was pacing back and forth on a discarded cardboard sign. Bauble could just make out the words—*please, fuck* and *food*—as he crossed back and forth. A taste in her mouth. The black oil of Sambuca. She remembered flinging herself around like a polyester tornado, loose cleavage swinging until that goddamned table had reared up in the small room's darkness. Such a moon out now, painfully narrow.

Ashley, wouldn't you like the moon to tattoo you? Imagine that, eh, being inked with the point of the moon, it would be so glowing. Who would look at me again if I had one of those? I'd be too bright, wouldn't I?

Shut up. Ashley had stopped, listening for something, then kept going, longer strides this time, all the way between the towers of baskets behind the door of the Kitchen Corner and the lamppost peeling with the skin of damp posters. The little girl was lying on her stomach, her oversize coat spreading around her as if she was melting. On the grate, the bottle rolled slowly. Dull, clinking sounds. Her hand slid small around the shaft of glass. A noise like distant iron fell from her lips.

Ashley dabbed at his mouth with one of Bauble's old make-up sponges, blood mixing with brown. *He's not coming*, he said after a while. Stood looking at the buildings, neon and brick, the stick-bare trees, the naugahyde emptiness of the barbershop. Then horns suddenly. The bright pop of fireworks over English Bay. *It's New Year's, baby!* Bauble shrieked, kicking up her feet in their blue fur slippers. The little girl rolled on her back, finding a few stars left to wink at her. Looked at the two of them from a distance, yelling *auld lang syne* with their arms looped heavily around each other, their lips, like a bruised language, meeting.

swarm

This here's my little girl. You show me a picture of something dark surrounded by frills, toys ringing her like a moat. *Isn't she hotstuff?* I nod. Your finger skimming the corners.

Hey, baby doll. One of the poolhall widowers with his paw around your butt. *Not now, Seppe, can't you see I'm showing off pictures?* Leaning on the arborite counter beneath the Starbrites, Saturday Night Fever. *This's my daughter. And where you been hiding her, eh, mamacita?* Seppe's hands with their softening calluses. Shoulders shrugging like eyebrows.

She's with her father, okay? In Terrace, where my people are from. But I'm going to welding school up there soon, Seppe, and then I'll see my baby for good. Fierce cast to your spine. Eyes withering away from you. I glance at the picture again. *She looks happy, Dara, anyway, healthy y'know.* Coffee lipping over the rim of your mug, tipping the edge of the photo. *That's not the point, though, is it?*

Turns to the cluster of men. Cards splayed upon the tabletops. Voices climbing with numbers. *Who's ready to go then?* Picture in your back pocket. Striding.

§

Wednesday at the Deux. Reggae night. Army boy slashing his rasta flag through the crowd, parting the dark sea of dancers. Beer swimming on the tables. You wear your plether pants. Legs like sticks of licorice entwining the man you move with. His glasses full of disco lights. *Mmmm, sister, mmmm.* Lips against your ear as your head tips back. Mouth split in a tight, high smile.

When you see me though, he plummets. Drops like a pebble into the deep pool of bodies. *Hi, sexy fiend!* Thighs snipping through the space between us. Arms clamped around my body, cunt thrust against my knee. *We be dancing, dancing, dancing queens.* The man you moved with tries to cut in. *Let's join again, sweetness.* Hands pry at us, futile. *Going to Babylon* with *Johnny Be Good. Could this be Love* and *You Don't Love me Anymore. Buffalo Soldier* like a *Lion in Zion. Three Little Birds.* When did I become your cage? Sex pressed against my bars. Light like broken keys spinning around our bodies as we sweat each other's softness far away.

§

In the Fall, the Natives tent for a week at Grandview Park to protest the loss of fishing rights. A fire by the playground spits in its ring of stones. You squat beside the Elders, a red band looping the arm of your suede coat. *This here's my little girl,* you are saying, the photo passing like bread around the circle.

It's been a while since I've seen you, but Manny, the local dealer, has been keeping me up to date. *Dara? That cat needs lotsa medicine. One time she set fire to my couch with her smoke she was tripping so bad. Then she got a job helping the guys roofing and stuff. So I let her come around again. Last week she brought a book with her. Whatcha reading, Dara, I asked to be polite like. And here it was this big motherfucking molecular physics thing she said she was almost through! Then she pulled up her top til her tits popped out and before you knew it, we were at it again. Crazy chick. That girl just can't get enough medicine, I'm telling you man.*

Stray children skip around the insects painted on cement mounds. Between the spigots that shoot spumes at their laughing mouths in summer. *Got any money for bannock?*

You have cut your hair, dyed it white. Strips of colour bleed around your lips. On the long nubs of your fingers, a litter of silver rings. *Aren't you working?*

Yeah, but I got to send everything to my kid for her Mr. Potato Head and Little Miss Bubbles and the farm set where the cows really moo. But Don's going to marry me soon, so it'll all be cool. Well, when he gets out of jail anyway. I hand you a loonie and you pinch my cheek. *Tanks, chickie.* Drums begin their heartbeats, tangling with chants that rise out of bodies like smoke. You strut assured across the grass to rejoin the loop of others both angry and feasting. Your voice leaping distinct as water.

§

Want to hear my opera? You appear out of nowhere on the corner of 1st. Alou spinning his squeegee like a magician at us. *Hey cuties.* Smile so dark and chipped. *One of the arias anyway. I've been working on it while laying bricks.* Your body erect, terse as a whip of seaweed. Lips straining over animal-straight teeth. Nothing wavering.

> *My heart is as blue as the sky/since you left me, sweet child. /And my eyes are as lost as the sea/*
>
> *Swollen with their big-ass sorrow /oh, blue heart, blue old heart /how the sky cracks, broken*
>
> *By such endless rain...*

You grin when you come to *big-ass*, then trail the tune off in a warbling kind of yodel. People turn to stare at you. *Are you sure that isn't a country song, Dara, or maybe some Ella Fitzgerald thing?*

No damned way, kiddo. Indignance in your pose. Prancing off the curb as the white man flashes on. *You see, it's all how the breath comes out of you. In opera, it's huge, girl. So much space for pain.* And you cross outside the lines away from me, arms still gesticulating, shirt lifting over stretchmarks which sashay across your flesh like little spurts of lightning.

Open Letter to a Black Hole

For F.B.

I never got to meet your father. No. And we didn't take photos in the ruins of old Montreal as the snow fell on our combined darkness. Sometimes we want to be neglected because it inflicts upon us the sullen intimacies of childhood again.

The way you wore a suit says everything, a biography of fabric. Shirt hanging, cuffs loose, lapel stained with Lebanese sauce. Your tie, which you swore bore a pattern of polkadots actually sprinkled with the tiniest blue & red roses.

I watched your mother iron once, her mother wrap strands of gray thread around the pink jaws of curlers. It was her birthday and you asked her what she wanted. *A clean and sober grandson.* The coffee was too strong. I peeled my mandarin orange and spoke of dolls, illiteracy, the still-endurable weather.

Remember when we walked through the graveyard? You have no interest in the dead. In Vancouver, I stopped each tear with my mouth when you told me you would kill yourself. You promised me your Pentax. The Tang in your fridge. After this, I knew the violence behind the desire to be rocked to sleep.

We ate in the worst cafes: The Green Spot, Le Moulin Jaune. The chefs had tattoos on their arms, obscured by hair—submerged texts. Everything slid on the plates, unmoored. If there was a jukebox at the table it played Celine Dion, refused Pearl Jam. You leaned across to bikers, glam queens, asking, in reluctant French, *Tu as du feu?*

Your etched, itinerant hands. Eyes that stumble in their shadows.
I have never sealed up a letter to you.

Some gestures have no lineage.

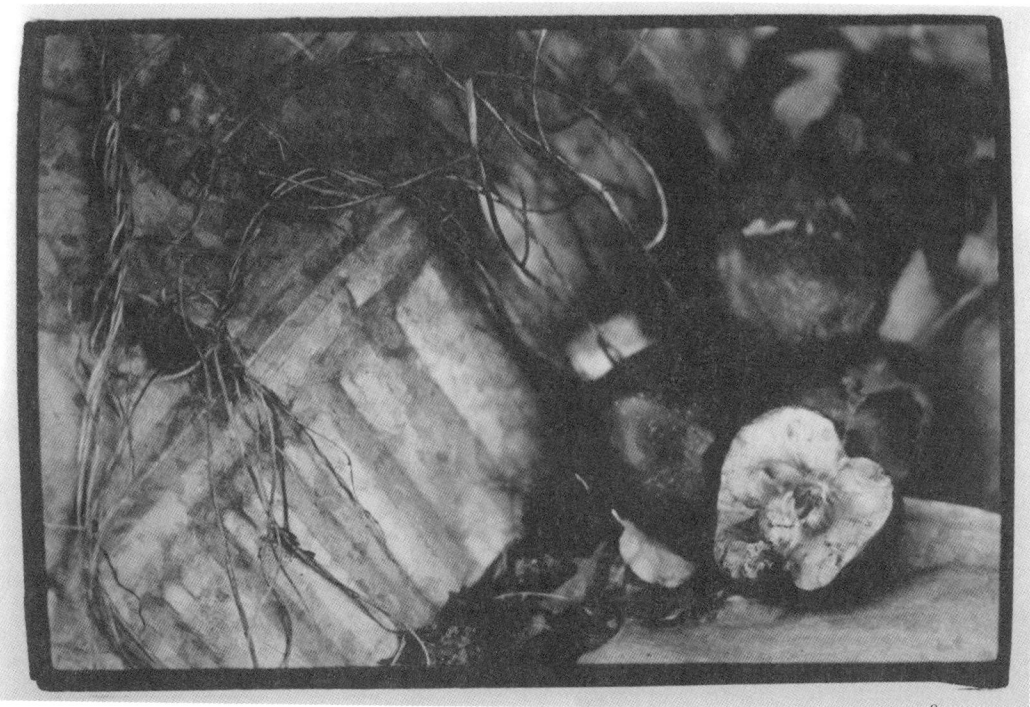

APPLES & TIN

No Water but Rock

Ma vie est dans la Montreal, ma vie est la—the knot in my gut cryptic at his voice on the answering machine, the machine of no answers for such familiar, distant utterances. In an instant, I saw his low income teeth, gnawed by smack, slightly bared between the low curves his lips made, his rarely-grinning lips. I saw his mouth pursed around a cigarette he'd bummed off a streetwalker, around a spoon that held the ravioli soup I'd reheated for him as he sat delinquently on the couch in my marriage of a living room. Saw his mouth around the over-nursed aureoles of my nipples, tugging drunkenly at the dry fount.

A month ago, he had told me he was going into rehab. Twenty-two days ago that he was planning to work as a photographer's assistant. Fifteen days ago that he had decided to swallow a gram of hash, ride the rails to a lawless American desert, see some cacti. He'd always wanted this, to know the feel of cacti on his palms. *Motion is your home*, I told him, stroking his illiterate, nicotined hands, the dark tracks of his hair.

After a while, after days on days, I heard from the needle-boys at H.H. that he was back at mom's, back in the arms of the corpulent doll-maker, back in the Hasidic, littered alleyways with Brothers 12 pounding in his ears, the pale, teen skin of his girlfriend within reach, his Pentax held to his obscenely wide green eye that had once been licked after a Husqavarna show at the Cobalt.

So much silence between us. I a thousand years older than him with my stretchmarks and manuscripts.

Mostly, I remember fluid. Not his semen knotted into condoms like the sad possessions of a tiny hobo, but the sweat I tongued off his forehead after our floor-hard sex. His tears also, those transparent nostalgias. And the fluid he poured from bottles into the low black trays he washed his seeing into light with, these most of all. The breasts and fists of unknown others breaking from the darkness like the forcefully-planted blooms of my life upon his.

dyslexic

You have no memory of how we met. Part of the problem is interpretations of daylight. There has never been a way for your pale crescent, a stranger amid the blue, to speak to my clamour of gulls as they rise in the steam from wood. The place I first saw you was dark. A room swollen with people. Your eyes like uncatchable species, tamed only by their shadows. I learned that you took pictures and asked what you first composed:

> *I was on a beach,*
> *years ago, when the light touched*
> *three round stones, a red, a yellow, and a gray one.*

Nothing ever called for response. As intimate as misery. In the weeks we spent in each other's company, my body became transparent. Sometimes it was a pool the stones of your words descended in, or a cellophane scrim upon mattresses and chairs. Sex was a tense space of forgetting, the sounds your pleasure made more a silence than your breath. Part of the problem is how we adjust to absence. Your refusals keep my words outsiders. Perhaps that is why I still write of you. We do not even share an alphabet. Your letters turn into their opposites, a child's irreverent blocks. If I could only stop being a translator for the invisible.

GHOST FENCE

remnants

I'm growing to understand your obsession with her. A feather and a stone do not travel at different speeds. She is a sliver of light, really, not female, not flesh. Or perhaps I am mythologizing her, as you do, to increase the mystery of my day-to-day routine.

You tell me how N. left you, how young she is, her particular vulnerabilities. Once she let a customer stroke her thigh because he said her eyes reminded him of oysters. Another time you caught her weeping because she had seen a fish cut open in the kitchen at Bouzyos bleed. *Green,* was all she could say when you asked her, *why isn't fish blood green?* There is a nondescript purity about her, as of something pared down to its reflection. Her cleft chin, the wary heat of her gaze spoke of so many unwanted ancestors. When you wondered if she would have your child, she looked at the dirt engrained in your photographs and declined, politely.

Now you too are leaving. Not to seek her, you claim. But who can know the sign of a shadow's immunity? As if trying to prove this, you have left me the pictures. Her on a street corner lighting a cigarette. Her on a roof, hair wet with the unexpected. Her naked. In the linked cells of contact sheets, I watch her body shift position, limbs like the film of a lily unfolding. I am growing to recognize your obsession with her. Absence. Its unbearable androgyny.

Dialogue for One Voice

If we had a baby, all I know is it would be gorgeous.

She doesn't answer. They are walking down the rutted lane. It is September.

But I'd have to call him Jimmy you know. And I'd teach him everything about stuff.

Her flesh already bears the skeins of a prior unraveling. She dreams sometimes that she has a child as dark and green as his body. A rat, made thin by countless wheels, presses its death into the earth.

My dad was a gangster, right. You think I'm kidding? And then, after all the shit he raised in the Cock and Bull, he goes and dies from some stupid tumor, like that, bang!

In her neighbour's garden, there is already wilting—tomatoes, figs. Rare, nameless flowers that spin their fragrance over the alleyway for a brief week in August. Someone has set a stuffed bear in the crook of an oak tree, its black button eyes glassy.

You think I'm joking?

She feels a tiny heat from his cigarette ash as he jabs her in the side. Playfully, she thinks. A crow on a streetlamp holds a lump of bread beneath its claw like a child that's been put to sleep.

I lived with my mother in the worst dumps and he didn't send me nothing. She made dolls with these huge faces out of old stockings. We ate lots of fast food, hot dogs and stuff like that. Except when she had boyfriends.

There is a house in this alley whose garbage is all art. A corset made out of wire, a statuette of a fertility god. This baby of cerulean clay with a gardenia for a head.

After I met my last girlfriend, I stopped shooting up, see. She barely knew how to make meals and I had to work, start wearing a tie. All the money we got, I used up taking pictures. Action photos mostly, empty and angry people.

Past the last ditch, there is a dumpster. A man pops up out of it like some toy from a horror film. She stares at him as he arranges his battalions of fingernail polish bottles, old tobacco tins and dented pop cans on the rim of this gaping box.

So why am I telling you this stuff ... so you know and don't like leave your husband or nothing to chase this bag of shit. I got this black negative cloud around me almost always, see. You like it now 'cause it gives you poems, but soon you'll be fucking running from it. I guarantee you.

There are purple, mouth-shaped flowers splitting up out of the cement by the movie theatre. She crouches down to count the yellow pistils inside, furzy with uncollected pollen. One bloom has even wound itself around the wire fence, almost painfully, to reach the light.

Crazy goddamned thing,

she thinks.

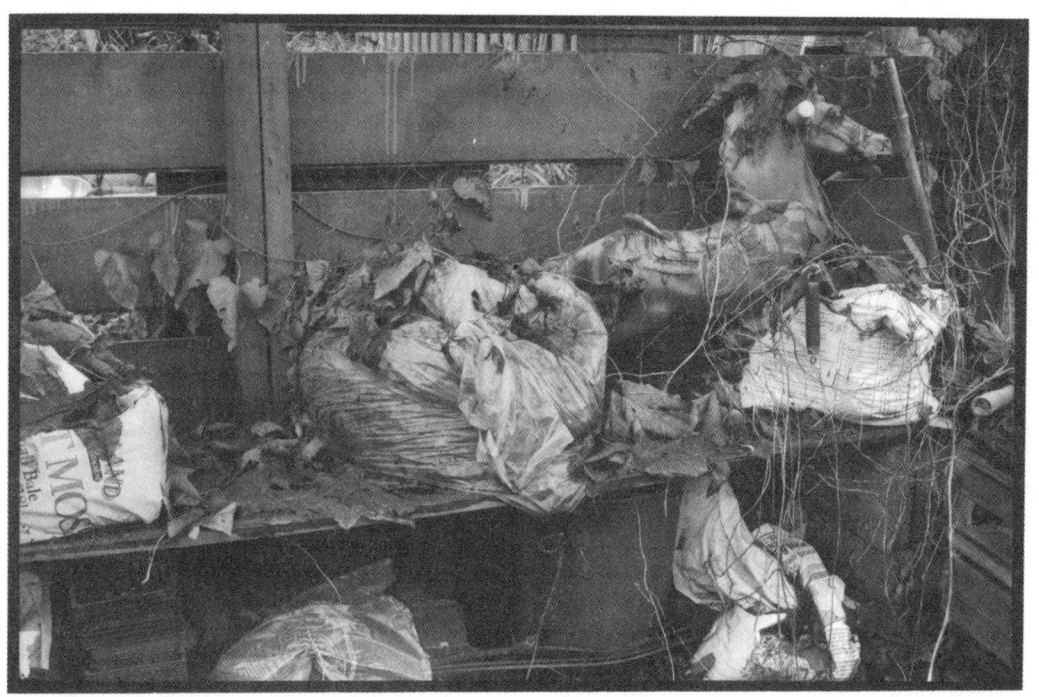

PLAY HORSE

The Hitler Room

Now that he was quite alone, condemned, deserted, as those who are about to die are alone, there was a luxury in it, an isolation full of sublimity; a freedom which the attached can never know.

—*Virginia Woolf*

Something was falling away from him. The Fuhrer was on television again, behind him the eternally whirling pinwheel of the Swastika. Arms saluting. Then a shot—the pale rubble of bodies in a pit, nakedness threaded together against the black seam of earth. *"It's all because he was a fucking failed art student, you know that right,"* Ken was saying to the raisin girl. *"Hey, have you read* Last Exit to Brooklyn?*"* He knew what was coming next. Even as it fell between his fingers with their fire-stains and smell of old photographs. *"Here, take a look at this."* The Book was being passed to her, the only book in the place, from the shelf beside the tilted mask, framed pictures of dogs, an empty treasure chest; above the bed, Ivan's bed with its mounted steel bar like the ones on the ferris wheel, his paraplegia recorded in the seismograph of sheets. *"Doesn't Frankie look just like Hugh Selby Jr. on the dust jacket here? Same big head, eh? Frankie, you know that's why I let you hang out here right, 'cause you look like my hero...man, what the fuck are you doing now?"*

He had been discovered. It was always this way. The gray sky chipping at the tips of skyscrapers; dogs pacing in their claw marks on the scrawny hardwood floor; Ken snipping at redolent masses of weed amid the chrysalides of rolling papers. *"Leave the fricking guitar alone! It's not mine so lay off it!"* Something had been loosened. Pieces of music swam in his hand. The wheelchair was missing screws. There were things lacking batteries, wires. *"Every time you come here, you mess with stuff."* All the parts were being snatched from him, stolen, taken away—"*to warmer climates, to feed the poor. Well, what can you do? Man, that's crazy. All I wanted was tea without caffeine and what do I get? Placebo city. Total Americana. World Domination. I gotta go to Lebanon. Trench warfare. Be a false prophet. Frankie-Jesus, man. Don't start this now, drive me fucking crazy. C'est l'enfer. C'est total hell. Jenny'll save me. The feminist diva. Huh. Now that is insane*"... (There was a wilderness of laughter in the room; in his chest; all the eyes were imprinted by his voice. His voice? God.

Something had fallen away from him). There were paper plates on the low table in front of the couch, remnants of *Soupe et Nouilles*, $3 ribs on them. They would do. They would ground him, keep him stitched together. A mantra churned in his body, roiling around a memory of calm. "*Ok, guys, I got a plan. Here's what we're going to do. See these plates here. We're going to meditate, arrange the blocks in our minds. These plates, they're the blocks. So watch carefully. No, first close your eyes ...*" (it mustn't escape him; the steps must retain their order). The room was dissolving into Dr. Boyd's words—"*Center yourself, Frankie, capture that energy and ... hold it ... hold it still for just a minute.*" Left, right. The Reich. The Reich. Left, right. The Reich. No, it was supposed to be all in a row at the beginning, yes, "*the blocks are red*" (the plates though were white with threads of sauce, dark veins). "*There are four of them, there they are. Can you see them?*" The bones shuddered on the plates as he moved them into formation. (He was no longer falling. The steps were finding him now, numbers sliding into his mind, digits goose-stepping). "*Ok, first examine the angles ...*" (but the plates were round, crimped at the edges. Trench warfare), "*then slowly pick up one block and put it beside the other one, not on top of it*" (even Ken was doing it; there were creases in his forehead), "*until a line grows, a four block line*" (he was keeping it together), "*side by side, and then, just as slow, grab one block, the one on the far left say and lift it up to the top*" (bones were sliding off; his wrist felt sticky with resin), "*then another*" (two plates were in the air now; he was keeping it together), *then the third* (balancing on his arm, perching level in the ridges of his sweater), *"and last ..."* A hand slapped his face like a cloud, hard against the moon's five o'clock shadow. *"That's enough crap man; the place is a shithole now, take your blocks and get lost. And don't come back 'til Ivan's out of hospital."* Plates and bones were soaring towards him. Stars piercing the room. The raisin girl's eyes were all starry like that Mötley Crüe song. *"Whoa, whoa, whoa, whoa, ooh, now, now, fucking Americana, man. I just wanted to go to detox and you give me caffeine. Who stole the patchcord? Who burnt the fucking meat? Hell on Earth. Can you believe them? What can you do? What can you do ..."*

He was puncturing through doors. He was teeming through hallways. Ken receding behind him into a splinter, black & white bomber planes falling endlessly through the screen, the Fuhrer's moustache speaking to him like a tiny animal, bleating its red language to a blank planet.

recovery

It had all started with the rich guy. Leaning back on the cot, sipping at the roach between his lips, he spoke escape with an easy whisper.

> *We'll put the sax in hock.*
> *My bass too.*
> *Yeah, your bass, and then we'll fuck off to New York, outta this nutzoid*
> *place and hang for a while, alright?*

Yeah, he had said, *yeahyeahyeah*, getting all worked up about it and everything. But then the guy had fallen asleep, hair slick on the green pillowcase. H. was left pacing his room on 4 East between the grilled door and the window overlooking McGill, burning with the walls around him.

> *Why am I here? Why am I still here when I'm totally stable and I've got stuff to*
> *do, the movie to write, the CD to record? Tons of stuff, man. Tons.*

On his way to the nursing station, he grabbed the ward guitar, held it behind his back like a bouquet. 1:00 a.m. or so. Crazies snoring, farting. Blood-speckle of lights.

> *Corrine, I'm signing out.*

No doctors around. They can't do nothing about it, he thinks, nothing. Wednesday. Smoke, watch TV and eat turds, that's all you can do here. Die in your greens like a shrine to Chretien or something. Shite.

Street clogged with people jockeying between bars. Would it be Fouf's or Chaos, Miami or St.Laurent? Laurent wins out. H'll be there with money for beer. He climbed the graffiti on the stairs, nudged the door open with his shoulder and there was Mike behind the bar, as always, ready to serve him his Rickard's, H playing pool with a tasty punker chick, greeting him, *Hey guy, what's up dude?*

Normalcy, fucking reality for a change.

§

Two or three. Time. Beer. Who knew? He had strummed on the guitar for them. Licks from his song, his best tune, "The moon means nothing to me." Two chords, but pretty-ass shit. The girl danced to it, then sat on his lap for a while and he fingered the holes in her nylons, getting a twitch in his drowsy cock. *Can I lick your eye?* she was whining, whining at him. H. kept sinking the white ball. Mike was wearing a pair of strap-on tits while he served them, fondling the rubber mounds with burlesque hands. *Goddamit, I'm bored again*, he thought, the coke switch flickering.

See ya H, see ya cunt, Mike, 'cause I'm going on the main, you better hide your cocaine… singing this as he busted down the stairs and into the June-ripe night.

§

The guitar was gone. Crap. He had sold it to some street kid for two quarters of the stuff that whumped his heart and left him hungry. *Gotta get s'more. S'more. S'more.* Pissing in the alley now, pants around his knees. *The human is but an animal in the final analysis.* Intoning this in a royal accent, huffing with laughter as he sprayed his initial on the bricks and it glowed a moment before evaporating. *Get me a gram. Get me a speedball. Get me a high so high that no straitjacket can take me down 'cause I'll be angel H with my wings of piss and sainthood, up over that cross on the hill, the false prophet of Montreal. Yeah.*

§

Woke where? Feet. Hands unmoving. Leashed to some flat hard thing like a cross under him. *Am I a caveman or am I a messiah,* he spoke into the green air. Lascaux mingling with Gesthemane. God, what was that stink? Then it entered him. Confinement. Back on the ward. Doctor's voice puttering above his prone body—*Cardiac arrest after that eighth of heroin you injected. Do you remember this, H? You could be dead. Dragged in off the pavement.* So now they didn't trust him anymore? It was straight down to Stage One again. No smokes and in the greens. Why the fuck? It was a sign of health, him wanting to shoot up, a goddamned glimmer in this steel-dull world. Nothing more than a beautiful cry for freedom, a needle-thin yawp over the thick-skinned rooftops of this nothing place!

temperature

Your eyes are like the way I feel when it snows. A child, melancholic with adulthood. When I was sixteen and pregnant, you used to stick snow pats down my shirt, palm-flat cakes of ice, pressing them between the new heat of my breasts, over the flesh-swell my belly formed as I screamed, tussling with your hands as though we hadn't just made the mistake of our lives. When it died, tiny and blue, blue as the strange light of snow, and you moved to Montreal, I distanced myself from the seasons. The first shoots of spring were little more than fingers shoved through the holes of gloves, ungainly, a discomfort. I viewed sand grains at the beach, autumn leaves beneath my feet, the way I saw crowds of people: aloof at their indistinctness. When you sent me a picture recently of you on a train,
traveling between Jean-Mance and Deux Montagnes, still looking as you did in grade school, although we are both now twenty-nine, I took one look at your eyes and knew your fathomless estrangement from winter. The only season I find in your gaze is a remembered one, and that itself is composed of unequal combinations of heat, and a cold below the barometer's relentless gauging.

UMBRELLA

eidolon

I think you have sent your messengers into the world. They do not speak to me in words, but their gestures lunge out at me from the unlikeliest recipients. An old man transfers your reticence before affection, a child the way your feet turn slightly outward like newly sprouted wings. Worse are those who replicate your shadow. Often they are derelicts, the city's closed shutters. In the streets, their bodies lengthen, eyes enlarging with a hunger I am hypocritical towards. I want to keep offering them coins so I can hear their mumbled utterances like news from a hardened country. Then, too, I want them to gaze up at me with the knowledge that I have nothing to give them, so the hurt settles on their eyelids in a dark snow. You are cruel to be so multiple. Even in my own flesh, your gestures stir their ghosts. I have gritted my teeth and become you. Tossed my head in agitation, chewed the pad of my index finger, sat legs open stirring sugar into my coffee with the lip of a spoon, and become you. Only eyes shut and smiling do I escape from all your messengers. Their attempts to convey your movement through my life, cryptic as the violent topographies of childhood.

essay

We grew together on the bed, in that hotel on St. Laurent, long in the gilded glass over the untouched sheets. Nine months apart had washed new scars onto our flesh. Thin horns fashioned a parenthesis around your knee from surgery's entrance. A welt marked the sun's scooped descent. But we were never skin and bone to each other, never cunt soft with want or penis mouthing from its shaft a sprung form of desire.

With our clothes on the floor like a disgorging sea, you thrust yourself in me as if tearing a Bandaid from a wound, as if our bodies would vanish from too tender a revelation of hunger. I longed to rend your mind and all its ghosts from this space for the hour I had laid down $20 for, slipping it towards the banal grandmotherliness of the concierge who had informed me that *malheureusement, nous avons pas une chambre pour plusieurs de temps*. Yet, like saying *Bless you* after a sneeze, or any gesture detached from its history of demons, this would have rendered you carnal and hollow with the beauty of any true lover. As it remained, I had only the knots you sacrileged in my laces, the small door of soap I stole from the dresser where, neat as any Bible, it was placed, and the knock, calling us away from the hope of assuming embodiment that still burned, somehow, in us both.

A Remedial Post-Mortem

For the last time, he was as a corpse to her. In the Bar Albion, surrounded by the ultra-French punks of the district, their frozen slogans crested with a Milky Way of studs, he sat, with his thirtieth Molson Ex, gripping it, rimming it as though it were flesh. [*she was steel/she was substanceless/she was the night air he had grown immune to*]. Sometimes he would rise, but it was only to slump over the slot machine and its spinning addiction of fruit, bars of gold, numerals. Once, in her attempt to reach him from the distances he had left her in, she had become complicit—"*black*," she had said when he had asked her—*black or red*—and then she had been a smart girl for an instant. This reminded her of the night before. "*Smart girls make me cum fast*" he had said when she asked why they always fucked so hurriedly, his fingers wrenching the roots of her hair or twisting her nipples until bright pain pierced through them as though this was the only way he could feel. When she had tried to break him of his blind, heatless motion by showing his hand how to move inside her soft dwelling places, saying *wait, wait for my orgasm*, she had only amputated him and it was a prosthesis she had thrust inside her over and over again, angrily determined. Crying out eventually with the strange, impeded coursings of her pleasure, she was only an infinitely tiny speech within him. In the Bar Albion, with its pool table, on-screen wrestling, and folk singer quavering to the irreverent, indifferent audience, there was him sitting. [*she was glass/she was absence/she was the day-moon he had consigned to be one of many insentient clouds*]. The time of his death, she then realized, had long since preceded her.

TEMPORARY

jagged

I watched my neighbour saw down his apple tree the other day and thought of you, trapped in your wheelchair in Sacre Coeur, growing out your facial hair to look like Castro. How many guises in which I have not known you. Vancouver—where the rain falls in spasms, thin shudders of drops feeding the roots of ghosted forests. I am here in a gray house. I am here whole in body. I am here as a detour into the one irreparable word.

A long time ago when I lived with you, in the hollow place carved out of Verdun's antique streets, pain was an imperative. By the time we'd slept together for a week, you had transformed me, as in a reverse fairy tale, into an image of your own misery. Scars and their small geographies littered my flesh, way stations of our walks and our fucking and your teeth. Sleep plastered its lack beneath my eyes. I marveled at how much you could withstand while still insisting upon immunity.

Where are we now, driver? called the half-blind man on the bus this afternoon as it jolted in mechanical spurts down the long circus of Commercial Drive. Some narratives cannot be repaired. The ones in which war is referred to as *peace time conditions*. The ones featuring women who have a fixation on *certain brutish numerals*. The ones whose characters speak in monosyllables and do not notice *the gauntlet cast down upon the parquet floor*. For weeks, the apples had been falling steadily. In the over-long grass, they turned up faces full of dark entrances and I pared them, with quick, uneven flinches, back to edible form. Reports from the front (but there is no longer any front; it slivers into our water, punctures the air) suggest that you wanted to be run over, sliced clean from the rank roots of your brain, its voices. That you lay down for the wheel's assuagement with the casual fever of a child waiting for his mother.

Watching my neighbour on his knees, sawing vigorously at the apple tree, muscles whole as soldiers, I imagine you beneath the machine, as many colours as something rotting beautifully. This is another thing you cannot feel, how my mind grows over every soft place on your body, trying, with language, to encompass it. The movement from bark to pith both possessive and indifferent. A catching of absence as it falls.

METAL & WEEDS

feather

I thought if I left him she'd fall asleep forever. As it was, when I asked him what his mother was doing, on the phone, in letters, he only replied with one word—*sleeping*—the sound sliding off his tongue like a sea bird into the chlorinated vat of water at the aquarium. I could see her refusing to leave her bed, pocked flesh becoming one with the sheets, the slack mallows of her breasts pouring sideways beneath her nightgown. Or she would wear a housecoat, zippered, as though she were about to rise, and slippers wedged on her feet, making you imagine her in kitchens, chatting with the ghost of your grandmother while she took nips from the decanter. This would be worse, you think, her decked out in these symbols of existence. "*When Francie were young,*" she would tell me, every time I arrived in Deux Montagnes, escaping my academic routine for the eyes of her only son, "*He thought he could fly. Not like most boys, you know, with the Superman thing, but real flying, like gravity was a plot dreamt up by teachers or something. Any of his little friends who told him he couldn't, he locked in the trunk, so's they couldn't breathe. Nearly killed Raymond.*" And she would gaze on his omnipotence with fond desperation until he said—*Ma, don't start*—stuffing his mouth with the poutine she had paid for with her welfare cheque. Then he would play the cheap organ in the TV room and she in her purple dress, her best one, perfumed and swollen as a crocus...

§

That's the way of our family, she might have said, when he told her I had finally refused his proposal of marriage, its unbearable coma of syllables, *flight's something we think only we can choose.* And as he slammed out of her house in his common refusal of mirrors, she would have preened those small white wings before falling heavily down in my mind where it runs & runs through its life.

The Curator

Nobody recognized him at the funeral. Such a mild man, a man made small by cancer, made old, sitting proper in his suit and sense of reserve, solid with irreversible dignity. His voice: dry, assured, chill as winter's endurance, a cold that has parceled the world into saleable fragments of snow. Up close, his taut skin flourishing its moles like nests in a barren tree. The word *gangster* whispers from him now, its sound, rich with the lure of Capone and Brando, unsure whether to still claim for its own this mild, small, made old man. You told me nothing about him. Once, in your apartment in Verdun, I noticed there was little in your fridge but a bag of miniature scones gone hard as fists. *"My father made them,"* you said. And another time, a salt-faced woman snapped—*"So she's the one!"*—in the rain on St. Catherine's and as we walked away you commented, *"My father's girlfriend."* This visit was to be redemptive.

§

"We're going to my father's for hot-pot." The hospital phone crackled and in the background I could hear Mrs. Flowers chanting—*"The line is curved and that's why Frank, that's why Frank."* *"Get back in your cell,"* you yelled at her. She whimpered and I heard her slippers shushing down the hall like a needle skipping at the end of a forgotten record. *"Yeah, so, tomorrow okay."* My silence registered the unraveling of a thousand improbable plans. *"Look, it's hot-pot,"* you said, *"it's gotta happen."*

§

When I came to pick you up you were sleeping, triangles of dress shirt and slacks sticking out from the back of a crocheted blanket. As I put the Pixies on the tape deck you awoke, rumpled and abrupt, kissing me roughly on the forehead, asking—"*Where's my rock 'n' roll shoes?*" Your father lived on Nun's Island, an upper-class enclave for retired Anglos. He had chosen his apartment, it seemed, for its lack of distinguishing features. Herod's soldiers would have been hard-pressed to determine which door they should strike with an X, they all looked so similar. The sea-eyed girlfriend served green tea while your father fussed about the kitchen, cutting long strips of meat, thin slices of zucchini, muttering in the sharp tones of impatience. "*You just have to let him do this, it's what he likes, you know your father,*" the girlfriend was saying in her coarse Brooklyn accent, "*such a stubborn man, wouldn't even go to the doctor until I dragged him in!*" You were curiously quiet as though cowed by the lush carpets, the armoir with its Toby jugs and china, the walls mounted with pistols, photos of countless golf games, the table arrayed with so many tiny, delicate mouthfuls. Your father presided over the meal like a general nervous about the finer points of his battle plan. "*Here's how you do it,*" he demonstrated, as he immersed a shrimp in hot oil, turning it from blue to coral with a few twirls of his fork, before scooping balls of rice onto our plates in precise formation. After dinner was over, I ate pie beneath the girlfriend's fluttering hands, while you asked your father for cash—"*Just two hundred bucks, so I can put a deposit on the camcorder dad, so it'll be waiting for me when I get out.*"

"*No, Frankie, you know I can't do that for you.*" His voice: detached, resilient, cement. "*But wait a minute, what I do have …*"

You returned from the bedroom with a bag. "*Socks, Kathleen, I have too many socks,*" your father said, striding ahead of you. Your face, as you clutched the lumpy gift to your chest, repeating—*this is my father and I am the museum of his life.*

O PARKING

list

List 1: Clothes I own

    Iron tie
    Burgody dress shirts
    Hemded cut off dress pants
    Grey & green swetters
    20 hole rangers
    Proletarian hat
    Skate shoes

He grew up in a house of women. Wantonly. Doted upon. Incapable of transgression (in the bathtub when he played dolphin; in the backyard when he played Superman). *Impossible*, Mrs. Flowers said, but Raimie, last of many hybrid and tyrant children, knew otherwise. He had seen (she sat knitting on the lime vinyl sofa in the smoking room) him raise an egg above his head like an aborted baseball and (sticking one hip forward, eyes sparking beneath his Expos cap) boast—*"I can do anything!"*—before (ten years old, unremitting, forlorn) smashing it down upon the tiled diamond floor. The horror! The horror! he remembered as yolk bled into albumen, shimmering and abandoned in a white archipelago of shards.

List 2: Things to buy

Green tea	Razor – cheap
Lemons	Shavecream – cheap
Echnecha	Dark choclate – lots
Ginseng	Viniger – small
Honey	Anis
toothpast	

You didn't believe him when he told you he'd make it all the way to Vancouver in that raddled Chevy Impala, 200 bucks and the hull bruised with rust, belching stench all the way down the road by the tracks as they left Two Mountains: he with bravado on the gas, she a sullen twisting through the fringe of dust on the back window. The trip remains a mystery to you, even now—what frayed hotels they stayed in, if they ate all the tins of Spam they packed. You only had a letter you received from him three weeks later, crowing—*At the Princeton. Lookee here*—folded over a photo—him in his zebra print wife-beater, slotted between the car and a dumpster, "Property of the City of Vancouver" on its sign. His face saying *will* and *chance* and *luck*.

List 3: Songs I've written

Misery bucket	twisted & free
Printed god	I can't hold a job
What if I don't want	don't wast your time
Simulated life	savage sun

"Give me the boy!" His voice, hard as barred histories swelled behind the barrel of a pistol. The wallpaper strained to martyr its smooth flesh but the women rushed like bees towards the burst door and rayed their bodies, indomitable, before the child who played on the floor. The gun-shaft waggled a clipped finger of lawlessness; the women's mouths rose in stratas of sound: shrieks, refusals, threats battening fast the loose wound of the house. His posse waited with the baby seat, milk and Pampers lifted from a depanneur in their sleekest heist. The child played on the floor, disengaged but for his eyes, old hives that held the swathes of what had made them.

List 4: To check in at hospital

    1 old bar bell
    1 pair combat pants
    1 pack sack
    1 winter jacket
    1 wallet (locked in 420-D valuables)

Among your possessions, you kept an essay from the dead. "Toi et Moi" it was entitled, a lined page scrawled in childish red, an account for Grade 10 composition of your Communism (nascent) and your hair (débouts), dubbing you within apostrophes a 'freak', a dive (the teacher noted) onto the disastrous terrain of English. Seven years had passed since a tangle of sex and amphetamines had led to his needled absence: slight boy with a mohawk and a homelessness in his veins. Since then, everyone else became him, Nietzschean beauties fiendish for argument. You wrote him into screenplays as the sharp hero of St. Laurent. In songs, his name trailed its dark fabric through 4/4 time. You fucked him mercilessly in every irretrievable skin.

List 5: To Do for

Health – eat/exercise/ no drugs/stay home & work on things/rest
Work – go to UIC in St.Eustache & Berri/check papers/make good CV
Art – record Apr. 10/write/test camera

When he came to visit you in the art gallery where you worked—pastels by Mont Petit, faux Klees, Native ravens stretched against faint watery landscapes—you knew you had to tell him. Little Troll waited in the lounge while you beckoned him to the back, storage area for unsold stacks of art, coffee pot, uncarpeted coils of scent. He was jaunty that day, you told Raimie, busting through the door, calling—*"Hey, qu'est qui arrive!"* then, *"Y'gotta smoke!"* bee-bopping around the desk where you sat—your clean, smiling clothes, the gentle earnestness of your mouth. Nobody had known where to find him and so the news had lingered its itinerant tragedy. Now his shoulders, beneath your hands, quivered impatient as hawk-blades. *"It's your uncle,"* was all you had to say, *"it's your uncle"* and he became still as a cry that cannot find its target. *"Bobby'sdeadBobby'sdeadBobby'sdead!"* the words pelting together as his eyes enlarged their wilderness at you. All you could do was hold him close through the sharp heaves of his chest until blankness shuttered across his vision again—*"Y'gotta smoke!"*—he said and left you in the clutter of the room to your knowledge of the men who had escaped him, dying with the crash of every last hard mirror in his mind.

List 6: What I need to do on April 9

    sleep

List 7: My Tai-Chi Essentials

    1/ **Want softness and use the mind**
    2/ **Distinguish solidness & emptiness**
    3/ **Link all the joints to act as one**
    4/ **Stable, calm, loose & pure**

If these were someone else's last memories of you, language would not have to heal anything.

§

Perogies in my kitchen. 6:00 p.m. May or June. You cooked, frying them in a sauce. We ate squished against a corner of the table (I have so many books). You knocked over a chair trying to kiss me; we did not know how to be friends.

§

Be my mummy you yelled as we fucked. The idea of pleasuring me was raised, was untranslatable, was dropped. *You're such a comfort* you said after cumming. *Let's get married. It's too late* I replied, feeling nothing. Tears fell around your eyes. Tea spilled on my sheets as you drank. Ash spilled on my sheets as you smoked. I got up and moved to the couch.

§

Please leave today I said. There was a toilet paper roll in the toilet. Your fingers were a shade of yellow. Your face looked un-ironed. *Take these.* I gave you your shoes. Your coat. I gave you food from the cupboard. Mr. Noodles. Baked Beans. I put it in a garbage bag with tie strings. *Take it all* I said. *Please stay at a hotel. You're a fucking bitch* you called. Your spit nearly hit me but it hit the door.

§

After this, I walked to a friend's. Saw you in the alleyway off Charles. 4:00 p.m. Running the other way I still saw you in my mind. Steel leg limping. Bag hanging down your back. You called once. Said my name but I hung up. I breathed quietly when you were gone. I breathed. I breathed. I breathed.

PANES

itinerant

his eyes do not contain the world
they are dark as the heart & lungs

he flirts with himself, then grimaces,
as shiftless as the elements

hastily, he paces the alleyways, hair
black with an animal's plumage

his arms never stop keeping timelessness,
but like a bee poised on granite,

he is lost in the silence of pollen.

asp

The dog is licking your wounds
On a sidewalk in Vancouver
In August, thick with tourists

And their cameras' private winters.
The dog is squatting over you, its scrotum
Wildly swaying, as its tongue's strange instinct suffers

Over rings of cracking skin.
And you are pale as concrete
Cast against the black lab's coarseness

The earth's indifferent passage
A scar upon your mind.
What is left for me to give you, set

Beside this futile gesture, this creature's
Frenzied cleaning of each red & open eye.

SHRINK RECORDS

nathan

Because he is one with his shadow
Because of if & regardless
Because when I first met him he told me a joke about a nun
   & a druggie
Because he could never remember that I didn't smoke
Because Dostoyevsky was re-christened in his mouth
Because of hot-pot for $3.99
Because he had a dog named Pariah
Because his journal is as worn as a shipwreck
Because the landscape is lacking without his body
Because of without
Because he traveled through the prairies with the word *slut*
   inscribed on his chest
Because he once ate cereal from a styrofoam cup
Because of the terror of circumstance
Because of circumstance, its beauty
Because he sang like Genet wrote
Because he wrote like Piaf sang
Because no comparisons are genuine
Because of microwaved burritos served by a man
   in a mini-skirt
Because of the chrysalis of his sleeping bag
Because while we were playing pool, he drew his portrait on
the chalkboard instead of the score
Because he had a solar system of scars

Because his jacket said *I hate you*
Because of words
Because of the way words traverse the backs, sides &
   groins of paper
Because he longed to have breasts
Because he once wore a second-hand corset
Because he described a mind like a hymen
Because death was not a theory for him
Because of whatever & perhaps
Because dog food & pennies mingle
Because a rope replaced a father
Because the squat became a shopping centre
Because of Sartre's nausea
Because his eyes had no age
Because his skin was like water
Because I am other than homeless
Because I am other than at home with this

PANE #1

barred

It is autumn when you enter the lecture hall
—students adrift on the islands of desks,
      the professor ascending into speech—

a small boy in the clothes of the street,
gripping his dog by a long ream of rope.
      In your backpack (amid rigs & corsets,

a cereal bowl), Gide and Camus, Dostoyevsky,
Proust's *A La Recherche du Temps Perdu*,
      Genet's journal of jail.

You stand on the stairs and look around you
—disgust and a lostness in your gaze—
      and I grieve for the life

drained from language
and your fruit rotting furthest
                from the tree.

dismantling

> *all that does not shine in the light...is sided with death and the wild, and the homeless are kept from public places.*
> —ROBERT DESJARLAIS

The low-breasted woman pauses
In the middle of tearing up plaster
Walls, the dry furze of insulation
To lean through the fence and say to you—
*Soon, this'll be a mini-mall, won't
That be exciting now?*
The vacant lot silent around her.
Its life of flowers & stones.

She couldn't have known last winter,
Nor would have cared for the street boys who stayed here
After days of chilled panning for change.
Their graffiti breaks down in her hands
Into a language of exile, unrecognized.
The small room, right where she stands,
Contained her blind spot's paraphernalia.
Not the imaginable needles and orgies,

The runnel against the alley where they would shit,
But the carefully-made beds, the stash of candy,
A candle's three-flamed vigilance.
There are things obscured by your fluorescence, you
Wish to respond, nails littered
Around her feet from the ruin
But she is far from this commerce of darkness
—her common blueprints unfurling.

PANE #2

Empty Landscapes of Psychosis

—Norman Mailer

1.

Clots your visions, this city, dark
Nodes of paranoia—Christ colliding
With the Aga Khan between the two
Hands of the Father, the Holocaust
Recurring in Safeway among the Star
Fruit, government spies lurking behind
Depanneurs. Pacing Verdun's mined
Byways, you dream as balm this searing—
A land more brutish than Dali's beaches,
Sun harsher than Van Gogh's heaving

Skies. They find you on your back
Amid the cacti, mind dissolved down
To its essence, a single grit of sand, too
Scorched to again divide.

2.

Snaps your voices, this city, fast
Splinters of delusion. Headlines
Lunge against your eyes. On Hastings,
Traffic assails you, missiles of sirens, bang
Of gutted engines, debris shrieking
Its demise. Squatting by the coffee
Shop on 3rd, you speak a final image
Of winter, a land still and unmeltable.
A place vaster than Alaska
In Which you alone would exist,
Clenched in an amphitheatre of ice, only
The sound of your own heart echoing
Off the frozen roof, your mind forever
Released from its flood.

delusions

For F.B.

They have opened you wide as a Messiah.
Divided by dice like his garments, your mind lies in Montreal's quarters
While you quiver in St. Henri, divested.

No alien abduction, this, your fine, inscribed receptors portioned out
By government agents, forces threatened by your status as false prophet.
They want to prevent you slipping into Christ's tight footsteps,

Singing in Israel from your luminous, sutured brain.

§

By twenty-seven, you will become a doctor, record an album of love songs, write a screenplay about a drifter named Guillaume and ride a Harley across the desert, snapping pictures of cacti.

Twenty-seven is three months away.

Don't worry, it can be done, you say repeatedly while rolling your sixteenth cigarette of the day, immobilized by your fear of the sun.

§

Your eyes, gouges against the night, do not yet seek, as the starving,
a space in death's flesh.

§

My hands, which have been reading your body's braille, will remember
each raised place and speak you, deciphered & whole, to the world.

drought

and before hell mouth/dry plain and two mountains
—Ezra Pound

And those who watched that evening would have seen empty forms of retrieval. On a highway, north of Ottawa, pent in a heatwave for weeks. Cattle, strewn by the scorch, scarce now, but white. Delirious with the parch of tongue and mind, you were finding your way back. Two mountains from a childish land rearing in your sight, water teeming down their flanks like touch. Who would know you to look? Defrocked of all amulets, origins, shorn to the pale of the skin. Beneath a juniper bush, your shrine, melting in its heap of memory: box of negatives, your grandfather's hat (saved for fishing), the photo of his burly face, aswarm with a lake's halo, a suicide's scarf and the sweater, striped like a felon, long talisman against the voices in your head.

Slow mirage, this ...

§

Moistness poisoning your lips from the Benevolent Society's piss, you returned for your stash, only weight you shouldered from the engine's busted shudder, way back in a capital city ditch. Yet shrubbery paced relentless the immense gasp of the highway and your hands, scrabbling

beneath their awnings, pawed only earth, its raw mementoes, weeping ...

A Glosa on Four First Lines by Siegfried Sassoon

Winter light on green walls, greenish
Curtains. He had been pacing much
Of the night—the narrow yellow hall
Between end of the world & world's end—
Nurses' station in the middle like Lethe,
A white-pilled wash of nothingness.
Slumping near the window where many leaped
He drowsed and was aware of silence heaped.

No one awake, not Al, shoes hilled
Beneath the sheets, Cass quieter
Than morphine, Runt back in the padded
Room—white bulb, lack of shade—
Nose ring removed to prevent
The suicide of the dead.
He'd seen it all before; he wasn't scared
He primmed his loose red mouth and leaned his head.

Stage Four by now, a short while
Til release; he'd sign the forms again, pick up
His gear: stereo & guitar, *le Manifesto
Communiste*, a welfare cheque—enough
For an NDG walkup, a 3-and-a-half where
He could work, undisturbed, on
His screenplay—*La Vie Continue*—
He seemed so certain all was going well.

The moment shook. A voice burst
From his head—*the inheritance has not been*
Left you, jerk, blood's warranty's expired.
So this was it then; this was it.
He had a letter to write, quick—gone to Lebanon,
Seeking death's fix—but first the dried-out
Breakfast, a little milk, splash his face.
He stood alone in some queer, sunless place.

Tai-Chi on the Psych Ward, with Frank

You breathe out a suicide, in your pajamas
Rm. 415, lukewarm morning of the plastic gardenias.

You exhale ten years of this froing between
home and the remote spaces of tray & shower stall,

cubicle and smoking room. In these motions from Li Po,
his perfect exile from chaos, your mind begins to lighten,

learn into its body. You do not mouth
the names your convict-beauty

becomes in bending to the ground, or arching
from the floor in flesh's slow extension. These birds

shape no nests on the ward, 21st century, 10:30 a.m.,
just before meds, small paper cups. Yet their echoes

attend your memory, homage you tenuous, and you
breathe out, in their mercy, your father's bullet voice

and the dark.

Un Patient est Trouvé Mort: Haikus from the French

From *Le Journal de Montreal*'s report of FB's death

1. *a quitté l'urgence de l'hopital vers six heures hier matin*

: Yesterday morning
  I was not thinking about
  You, only, faltered

2. *il a eté avancé, a un moment donné*

: A given moment
  Your Chuck Berry shoes over
  The edge, black and white

3. *il a fait une chute*

: Taking a leap, you
  Thought better of it, falling,
  Or not, the air live

4. *sans armes a ses cotés*

: At your sides, your arms
  No longer, but flailing, stilled
  —A fist shooting up

5. *en bas du stationnement*
a l'étages, étendu sur le dos

: On your back, they told
Me there were no wounds, no blood
—Your casket opened wide

6. *la corps de l'individu,*
au beau milieu d'un vaste
éspace de stationnement vide

: An empty lot, vast
With asphalt, your body broke
The traffic, always

7. *le cadavre d'un homme*

: A man's corpse, you or
The man you saw as missing,
Sheeted for the lens

fix

into your pocket in the sharp stall you placed
(how many draws?), the coins from a quarter
gram, two pennies & a nickel whose queen
floated in her silver ring, features illumed and
indifferent. i will not imagine the needle's
moment but the quick unwrapping, 3- by
5-inch paper in which the junk sat in its square
stain within a field of numbers (would you
like the Extra?), gray scent clinging. into your
pocket the piece slid before the vein and
the coroner said (Play Lotto Quebec) *"here
are his last possessions."*

PANE #3

The Laying Out: A Glosa on Lines from Osip Mandelstam

On each stair a flitch of snow and more snow
falling. They move ahead of me: Maria,
Freddie, and your best friend, winding
through the clefts of tire tracks that
split the road to the funeral home.
A marquee beside the door holds your name.
I trail behind to trace each letter—the
first and last gesture of your life.
Everyone else has gone inside.
I am alone staring into the eye of the ice.

§

*Pas responsible pour objects perdu
ou volez* reads the sign in the vestibule
above the dark shoal of coats. People cluster
as at a *vernissage*, in reddened knots, chatting,
hands clutching cups or napkins, eyes
gazing at walls. I make my way down
the hall towards you; as if I were your wife
they step aside. This lie that nothing eases.
I am haunted by a few chance phrases.

§

"He was ready to die;" "This is what he wanted;"
"At least now he's in a happier place": words
circulate with albums and condolences.
I look at you from a distance—everything
is wrong: the suit, padded & brown, the silk,
the frills, your face, made up like a neglected
doll's. It is not death that has changed
you, this familiar that you sought, but
the strange artistry you've become.
I could not keep your hands in my own.

§

And so the coffin holds you: undiscriminating,
motherly, attentive. The fluid in your veins is not
blood; your shirt hides further scars of entrance.
Who are you without your tattoos, smoke
trailing from nostrils, hair tussled
upwards? Memorabilia of flesh
I weep over, though in weeping
is no redemption for your leap, nor
one chance of drowning back to life;
I have to live, even though I died twice.

PANE #4

The Mourners

Myrna:
Envious of tears, eyes blond & red clench against themselves. "I'd cut him off lately, well as much as I could, forgot to worry, a relief, but now?" Under her pillow, his face becomes an icon: enshrined in chrome, clean, not lunging from the couch, screaming, tobacco-yellow. Yet public weeping denies its balm; disdaining the globe I place on his Maybellined cheek, she rolls a banner, black, from the U2 concert of youth, places it beneath his incongruous silk—"so damned dramatic"—she dubs me later.

The Giant:
Wrestler-girthed, got up in an unworn suit, riding inches from the wrist, yet sharp, concealing the Coq d'Or grease I saw him wearing last when you dragged me for a *tisane et du boeuf avec des patates*; the continental splats on his apron, Angus Young tattoos blaring, hidden now as is the *bonhomie* of his youth—"I can't believe he's gone."—aimless around the room, crying into the meat of his hands.

The Stepmother:
Bred in the Bronx light of a department store, the blank circuitousness a gangster's palisade requires, you are snappy with caresses, dunking a tea bag into the plumbed depths of Styrofoam—"You gotta keep it together for her."—you caution me, nodding to his mother as though your desert serves a firm stitch to her loss. "It's obviously what he wanted."—grief's ceremony shortened to a cursory sigh over youth's Expos games, pop raised, goofily grinning—"He was so happy then, but ..." her purse coffining shut, "things change."

Gallery: Anti-Sonnets

FRANK'S PHOTOS (1994-2001)

    machine: Thick wedge of chrome.
           Yankee appliance you can see
           Your face in, wonky, stretched
           To breakfast advertisements for
           Dripping on brown, jam on white.
           Yet what pops up is not an Eggo,
           Its blond half-smile, but
           Circuit boards, the crusts cut off
           Harsh electric squares
           Threaded with science.
           Does it feed us, what we enshrine,
           Call solid and complex and epitome
           Of human? "They've poisoned my food," you say,
           Your hand shrinking away, your face.

          La belle dame sans merci: a lily on thy brow and on her
                             thighs, angled away from your gaze
                             like swans a lily the light of her skin
                             cast upon the Man Ray waters black
                             the backdrop black the pageboy cut
                             of her hair and her eyes were wild
                             charcoal-thick as rushes on the cold

        hill's side closed as the mass of her lips
        a child's sash her nipple a child
        waving from the hillside cold
        and unredeemed body lengthening
        away from your lens the holes in her flesh
        no refuge but winter where no birds sing
        and fugue, desire, refusing.

Clash: There is nothing of the Old Masters
       Here, yet the mind still strays to fragments:
       Caravaggio's "King Solomon," Vermeer's illumed
       Women, a conflict lifted to stone.
       You saw him first in St. Urbain? The pitted
       Anachronism of his cheek, the young punk
       He was hassling, his friend's Gorgonned-sneer,
       Ça blonde's queer pertness. A metro ticket
       Unpaid? The collision not the issue but a
       Raw inversion of images: pure punk, nasty
       Cop, etched sharp against a gyre
       Of buildings. What you wanted to
       Understand, the way you scoured for battles,
       Seeking the borders of dark and light unsettling.

needle: His head is in shadow like a stabled
       Horse, dropped as if to bunt, teeth
       Gripping the bit (a seat belt), the sun

Eclipsed on his shirt. You would have had
Me witness you too in this act, begged me to buy you
Coke—"You'll get a poem for it."—you said, knowing
The indifference of the artist's hunger. But I
Declined, for once putting your hell
Before my need to see. You
Did not lose your duty, but clicked the instant
His fist unclenched, the needle entered. Above
The tattooed spires, his vein swinging like a jockey's gate,
The mad liquid galloping to its end,
Syringe descending, spent.

Smashed Plant: In the *salle de bain* of the Polytechnique,
        The man, hard as Atlas, strips.
        His head is buffed white as a summer
        Afternoon; his muscles gleam; his sex
        Is soaked in shadow. The eyes
        Of the porticos watch. He used to have
        A plant between his hands. He used
        To be in the picture. But the sequence
        Has unrolled to its finish as if a dark
        Ribbon of history; the descent has been
        Accomplished and now the plant
        Lies on its side as though it had uttered
        Nothing. Small granules of dirt, roots
        Limbed from the pot; the gallery of your mind, looted.

negatives: Either they were found or they were
              Not found: the box you forgot
              On a highway north of Kenora
              As the ambulance sped your dehydrated
              Flesh to an amnesia of healing. Either
              They were found—their shadows washed
              In light, pinned on lines like strange fruit,
              Exhibited as *anonymous, route 95*—
              Or they were not found—dark squares
              Reflecting no filtering face, each season
              The heat bleeds them, the damp roots in them
              Until they all become images of earth. These
              Negatives, these fragments of your crowd;
              Either they were found or they were not found.

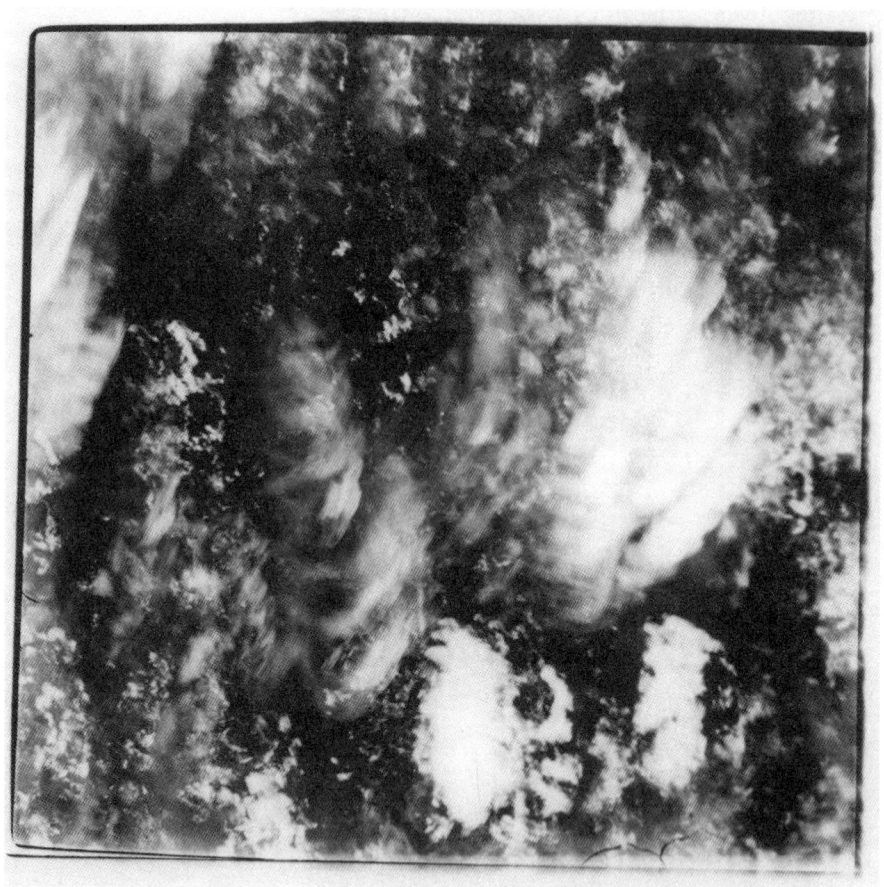

WIND

The Ward

Madness being the point of contact between the oneiric and the erroneous
—MICHEL FOUCAULT

Presuming to be the scribe while you live the agony
—MARGO BUTTON

Child of the green air, of the lust for syringes in the sky above Verdun's caustic alleyways. Child who donned a cape to fly through glass. Child inside the child inside the trunk when it was dark and the airholes were as tiny as whispers. Child of the time. Child of the palms spilling with gin. Child whose flowers grew like burns. Child of the trip between school and the moon. Of the scars on the shin, child, of the Milky Way of chains. Child whose pills as the mouth of sleep were white and round. Child who lived outside the frame. Singing child, flesh etched into the strings. Child wrapped in a sheet whose feet stuck out like memory. Child who has cried in hallways. Child of the mind on fire with voices. Of the ashes, child of my haunting. Dear god, this child of the eyes.

§

    Like a fly grown tall as a door, the hill
    Bruted itself into a hospital. Two hundred
    Years after Bicetre, Scipion, La Pitié

Moored the Ship of Fools in a dock
Anchored by rankness, dark bricks compiled
Themselves. Insanity enables

Architecture: stairs leading to nowhere,
Corrugated walls, labyrinthine incarnations
Streaked with yellow tape like straw.

The fourth floor no different perhaps
Than other wards, while unacknowledged
By the elevator, and with a scent

Transgressive to sanitization:
A queer, curtailed wandering to the halls.

§

who is this you	I have found and fear
always to lose	a mind-frond ridged
similar to mine	yet torn more easily
primeval	frayed by language without
junctures	unstable as the last moon's
roots	who is this you woven from
a homelessness	acknowledged and storied
an affinity	with what undoes us at night bred
in your	day-flesh and so

silenced   by meds   and so silenced   who
is this you   lunging   from the bed
to greet me   cocooned   on your side
un-butterflied   weeping from
the voice   in your dream casting the glass
at strangers   brightened with your sweet punk
singing   who is this you on the highwire
my face   catching   your every gesture
yet incapable   of containing
your fall

§

No holy locus this nor ever was
Such a place, though stabbed
With the gist of Christ—

Pallets of shit below crucifixes, hymnals
Cupped like water. In Bethlehem,
A man was found who twelve years

Had been chained for refusing
The Prior's consolation.
A sign of recovery being

The return of discourse from
Delirium
To the beast-less plod of the Word

§

J'en voix les diables! old creased voice   like a handkerchief
sepia toned   oval as the virgin on the wall   Jesus
pacing in your skull   evil as his fountain   of crosses
toss on the rubber sheets   speak a talisman language against
the darkness   *les diables*   beneficent as nurses   but with tiny
bricked eyes   and pills lodged beneath their fingernails   you have
named me the Sun-Maid Raisin girl   affixing a torn
portrait to your tongue   sitting on your right-hand side
ordained while Billy Joel sings the tune   of salvation
only the desert can save you   with its white-robed sand   and
sky devout as the hour your mind burnt its insignia onto the charts
ten years old   the coven of doctors noted   wild as icebergs
around your bed   the silence never since then an option
in the animal recesses of your head

§

At Bicetre (as it was in the beginning) madmen
Were displayed: splayed limbs, eyes agog, trained
Drools (so shall it be), dances feigned by whip

Or tidbits dangling from a mobile of hands.
As late as 1815, a penny was the going rate
To view such cruel tableaus, the money

Clenching its own tail in a circle of viability
And reform (world without end). So many
Visitors cycled through the spectacle

It was as if their hunger for nightfall
Had no means to be abated (amen).

§

Dreamt door became an almighty fly   washing its silk disease against
my glass with long black licks   the window is seamed
with legs that dwindle   in diamond shapes   and the wood
splintered   as lips   kissing always into the distance
two white cups like geese   beside my bed   carry on their backs
dark notes   not songs like *Love Me Tender*   but scripts
not for *A Streetcar Named Desire*   but thin soft waverings of night-
like reminders   the patchcord left in the trunk   the meat burnt
the cunt not hollowed   with nicotined fingers   until it is a puppet
you can talk to   slight and nodding   as a sunflower
notes like this   or the doctor's illegible speech   *take the silent pill, son*
or the one that makes   my tongue   lunge   broken
eyelids swell like the sun going down   skin worm   unreadable
dreamt dances   chained to bedpans   applause of piss   around
my ankles

§

Pain (as the fish's blood is cold) once
axed from the attributes of the mad,

is never re-instated as absolute. Nor cold,
heat, nor hunger, work their way
into the records, so that women, naked

in below-zero cells, seemed *impervious*
to the climate while men yoked
to plows were said to labour hours

beneath the harsh sun's whip and want
for nothing but further punishment.
Treatment proceeded from this illusion

until the body became but an appendage
to the animalized mind.

§

who has seen the stigmata on your shoulders threshed
by the rays from the time you lay   face down
on the road in drought while your voices teemed
like geysers the sharp mask your ribs wore
when weeks the food was poisoned the tremor

the blue night   you found refuge   in a boxcar who
has heard   you say   *I know l'enfer*   *and it is both*   *fire &*
ice   *both the slow*   *parched leak of breath*   *and pain's*   *swift*
icicle entrenchment

       §

    Apophany, the effulgence around objects,
    a hagiography of the everyday (comb,
    toothbrush, water glass invested with locutionary

    powers), the recurrence of the eye, the I's
    bastion of voices, all these leashed
    in the modus operandi of the ward.

    Once, a doctor would appear
    as the dead, Beelzebub, a prophet, speak
    to the mad in their own language, seeking

    to turn them from visions with a brute
    inversion of their own images. Now
    awakening is favoured through the durable

    routine, a certain time for breakfast, therapy
    after tea, lights out at nine. Further methods
    selected by frustration—the subtle infliction of pain,

    anger inflected in requests, a nurse yelling

parasite!, hoping to cast a mirror
that cuts an anchor in the face.

§

Parasite!   Genet's lice in his clothes   an aliveness to his flesh
squandered by a century   of clean   zeroes pinned on the line   like
gutted moons   ciphers washed like chalices   who in a dream stands
unsuckled   night not the vector of thought   never asked to live   in Gethsemene
to coil in the garden like a root   its tree gone Judas on him
her mind against mine so rank   I have choked in its sour-blind scent
the curt   crawling word of her mouth   til I am world
no longer   but runt   maggot of the rut in the floor   plotting
deliverances   devourings

§

The void of Goya's madhouse,
flesh groveling in the hold—
to be Captain of cigarettes!

To dole out the saviors
in a room yellow as the endless
yammering tide! This is ordained

as act. Or cleaning your plate.
Receiving visitors in public. Quiet
masturbations in the bath. Correctly

taking down phone messages. Making
your bed. De Sade at Vincennes
burning his flesh to the ash of art

would likely now cost him a straitjacket
or a slot in psychiatry's Most Wanted.
There is a piano provided in the lounge

but its tunes must be simple as speech
from which all of the screams
have been gutted.

§

to make not-silence   I have tin   the polished wood of Orpheus
keys   drenched in silver   and a reed   I name
my backbone   in this way I am a whole   clang of people
asserting   the dawn   art's negation   in their uniforms
in the smooth white moons of their mouths   speaking pill upon pill
in monotone   the voices too   neglect   the film
the tilt of the firmest paintbrush   forget the dialogue   scrawled
between characters   in a St. Denis coffee shop   seems

only moments   in life   there is balance
when one sounds outside of all chains   and in the mind
still reversed   by night   hear me chiming.

END NOTES

The Midwife . . . . [Randall Deere, is a 27-year-old street prophet/schizophrenic who can still be found roaming Commercial Drive in search of change. He also appears in "Exhibits (A)" and "Empty Landscapes of Psychosis".]

Exhibits A, B, X . . . . [Quote from: Louis Sass. *Madness and Modernism: Insanity in the Light of Modern Art, Literature and Thought.* New York: Basic Books, 1992.]

Open Letter . . . . [French trans.: Do you have fire? (ie. a light?)]

No Water but Rock . . . . [The title is from TS Eliot's poem "The Wasteland." French trans.: My life is in Montreal, my life is there.]

The Hitler Room . . . . [Quote from: *Mrs. Dalloway* by Virginia Woolf. French trans.: It's Hell.]

List . . . . [this poem features actual lists from Frank's drafts and scrapbook.]

List 3/4/5 . . . . [French trans.: grocery store/messy or sticking up/What's going on?]

itinerant . . . . ["jitterboy" is a mute schizophrenic who can be found striding down Commercial Drive or sitting at Juicy Lucy's over innumerable cups of coffee. He also appears in Exhibits (B).]

nathan . . . . [a 19-year-old artist from the Prairies I met in Vancouver in 2000. Other poems featuring him are "current," "asp," and "barred."]

dismantling . . . . [Quoted from: Robert Desjarlais. *Shelter Blues: Sanity and Selfhood Among the Homeless*. Pennsylvania: University of Pennsylvania Press, 1997.]

drought . . . . [Quoted from: Ezra Pound, "Canto 17".]

A Glosa . . . . [Quoted from: Siegfried Sassoon's *Collected Poems*. French trans.: Life goes on.]

Un Patient . . . . [Quoted from: *Le Journal de Montreal*'s report of Frank Bonneville's death (March 1, 2003).]

French translations:
Title: A patient was found dead
#1: He left the hospital in haste yesterday morning at 6:00 a.m.
#2: He ran forward, at a given moment
#3: He jumped
#4: Without his arms at his sides
#5: He was at the bottom of the parking garage, stretched out on his back
#6: The body of an individual, in the centre of a wide space in an empty parking lot
#7: The corpse of a man

The Laying Out . . . . [Quoted from: Osip Mandelstam's *Collected Poems*.] French trans.: Not responsible for lost or stolen objects/art exhibit

Gallery . . . . [Quoted from: "La Belle Dame Sans Merci" by John Keats.] French trans.: Washroom

The Ward . . . . [Inspired by and quoted from: Michel Foucault. *Madness and Civilization: a history of insanity in the age of reason*. New York: Vintage Books, 1988. Margo Button. *The Unhinging of Wings*. Lantzville: Oolichan Books, 1996.] French trans.: I see devils!/Hell

"The Ward" was written after a week spent in the Montreal General Mental Hospital with Frank Bonneville. Frank was born in 1974 and grew up in Deux Montagnes, Quebec. His father was a member of the infamous West End Gang. Frank played bass in the death metal band, Eulogy, for singer-songwriter, Biffy Perdu, and mastered all the instruments/ vocals for his own label: Pretty Girl Music. He had a diploma in photography from Dawson College and interests in screenwriting, tai-chi and capoeira. At the time of his suicide, Frank was struggling with drug addiction, schizophrenia, and grief over the deaths of his best friend Luke, seven years earlier, his grandmother, a year previous, and his uncle's sudden heart attack just a few months prior. Frank can be found throughout Cusp in poems such as: "Coroner's Report," "Exhibits (X)," "Open Letter," "No Water," "dyslexic," "remnants," "A Dialogue for One Voice," "The Hitler Room," "recovery," "temperature," "eidolon," "jagged," "essay," "A Remedial Post-Mortem," "feather," "The Curator," "List," "delusions," "drought," "Empty Landscapes of Psychosis," "A Glosa On Four First Lines by Seigfried Sassoon," "Tai-Chi, On the Psych Ward, with Frank," "Un Patient est Trouvé Mort: Haikus from the French," "fix," "The Laying Out: a Glosa on Lines from Osip Mandelstam," "The Mourners" and "Gallery: Anti-sonnets."

He has served as a primary inspiration for my own art and that of many others, including his friends: Rich, Keith, Gary D., Gary C., Nicole, Tom, Tracy, and Jay, his cousin. Other people who were important to him are: Jenny, Lorna, Lara, Aaron, Pam, Jasmine, Scott, Joel, Alex, and The Reverend. My thanks to Debbie and Frank Sr. without whom this dark lightning would have been lacking from all of our lives.

Acknowledgments:

The following poems have previously appeared in:

The Midwife (*Quills*); jagged; temperature (*The Fiddlehead*); remnants; eidolon; Once Upon a Space (*Dandelion*); Open Letter to a Black Hole; An Astronomy Lesson (*ARC*); Coroner's Report; Tai Chi on the Psych Ward, with Frank (*Event*) The Ward (*Poetry Salzburg*).

Eight poems from *Cusp/detritus* are also included on the same-titled CD (Krisananda Music, 2001).

Afterword

Elegy for the only

The day your death cracked
Through the asphalt line dividing us
: West from East, lost from the living, I
Recalled a dream the night before

The needle's imitation where you spoke of love
In your voice of dark trees. You'd said
Words would never again sing between us,
Never singe us in insults or admissions of need

—But never were you twin to silence.
Who can consign you to the earth's quiet burial?
You will always be walking with me

Through the McGill Ghetto as we did
Last Spring, flanked by the Garys and Tom,
Kicking a can in simple elation (brief
Shining in a mind of deserts), crying out

Raw, unabashed, laughing—

Vive le Frank libre!

Karen Moe and Catherine Owen

ABOUT THE AUTHOR

CATHERINE OWEN is a Vancouver based poet whose work has been published in national and international journals such as *Queen's Quarterly* and *Poetry Salzburg*. Her first book *Somatic: The Life and Work of Egon Schiele* (Exile Editions, 1998) was nominated for the Gerald Lampert Award, while her second collection, *The Wrecks of Eden* (Wolsak and Wynn, 2002) was shortlisted for the BC Book Prize; a third, *Shall: Ghazals* was published in the spring of 2006. Her work has also appeared in the anthologies *A Practice of Spirit* (St Thomas Poetry Series), the SFU compilation *Companions and Horizons* and *Essays on Joe Rosenblatt* (Guernica Editions). She has a Masters degree in English and is the singer and bassist for the blackmetal band, Inhuman.

ABOUT THE PHOTOGRAPHER

KAREN MOE is a Vancouver photographer and multi-media performance artist. Her shows include *perros y leones de centro habana* at the Havana Gallery in Vancouver in 2002 and Pteros Gallery in Toronto in 2005; and *Lethe: a mock-metaphysics* at Xchanges Gallery in Victoria in 2005. Moe's work also graces books and album covers, and has appeared in such journals as *Dandelion* and *West Coast Line*. The *detritus* pieces were exhibited at Exposure Gallery in Vancouver in Spring 2005. Her CD, *Stoic Pharmacy*, will be released in Fall 2006.